To Grandfather Daniel Komarek

ristmas
(1967)

THE WHITE SANDS INCIDENT

OTHER BOOKS BY DR. DANIEL FRY

Steps to the Stars

The Curve of Development

Atoms, Galaxies and Understanding

THE
WHITE SANDS
INCIDENT

by

DANIEL W. FRY, Ph.D.

BEST BOOKS INC.
1900 Bashford Manor Lane · Louisville, Ky. 40218

Dedicated To
My wonderful wife Tahalita
Whose prayers and constant aid
Have helped so much to develop Understanding

Wisdom is the principle thing
Therefore get wisdom
And with all thy getting
Get understanding.

Proverbs 4:7

Contents

Contents

Introduction

THIS is a true story of an unique event.

Some will believe it—exactly as it is written—and those I sincerely want to thank for their belief. Others will smile and say, "It sounds interesting, but I don't believe it."

Yet, believe it or not, on the evening of July 4, 1950, I had the experience of seeing, touching and riding in an unmanned, remotely controlled space capsule which landed near the White Sands Proving Grounds outside the city of Las Cruces, New Mexico.

I soon learned that this amazing vehicle had obviously been created by a technology considerably more advanced than any known to exist upon this earth.

No public report was made of this event at the time it occured; partly because the United States Missile Proving Ground, where I worked, operated under a tight "security cover."

In addition, the nature of the event was, to most

people, so incredible it seemed unlikely that any significant number of persons would accept the report as anything but fantasy.

In 1954, however, I was persuaded to make a public report of this event.

Because of the great social and technological significance of the arrival of this extra-terrestrial device, I was led to believe that the public was entitled to know it had occurred. And I was convinced they should have access to the technical and scientific data which was offered by the "operator" of the space capsule.

Unfortunately, factors involving the rules of military security prohibited the publication of a large amount of the specific data I received.

Twelve years have now elapsed and the factors which prevented the publication of a full report at that time have run their course and the full story can now be told in greater detail.

Those same twelve years have seen a tremendous advance in our own space technology and the accuracy of many of the statements in my original report has now been demonstrated.

Because the information contained in this book is true, many readers will accept it for what it is—an account of events which actually happened.

Other readers, however, may not accept this account as fact, but they will find within its pages many things of interest. And much of the information will,

2

eventually, prove to be of great value to our present day scientists and to the nations of the world.

In the meantime, I have been asked to go on a coast to coast tour to appear on radio and television and give lectures on the subject of U. F. O.'s (Unidentified Flying Objects) and I would like to invite you to attend one of my lectures whenever I am in your vicinity.

Questions are always asked after the lecture has been given and I am sure some of the questions you have in mind will be asked—and I know you will enjoy hearing the answers.

In September, 1963, it was my privilege to speak to the entire faculty of two school districts in the southern part of Oregon. The lecture contained a number of statements of great interest to those who are concerned about the future. The *Medford Mail Tribune,* the daily newspaper of Medford, Oregon, reported the major points as follows:

" 'There are students in our high schools today who will stand upon the surface of Mars and Venus before they are 30,' said Dr. Daniel Fry, a scientist and former missile engineering executive, in a talk for the teachers of Medford and Ashland schools yesterday.

" 'We must do everything possible to prepare this generation for what it is going to do,' he told the teachers. 'We are going out into space, and we must be prepared for what we will find there.'

"Fry went on to voice the opinion that earth beings

will find intelligent life on other planets. 'It is statistically certain,' he said, discussing estimates made earlier this year by a Harvard astronomer, 'that at least one million planets in our galaxy attained the ability to travel in space two million years ago.'

"The speaker addressed a group of 500 at Hedrick Junior High school yesterday morning for an hour, and then spoke for two and one-half hours for 140 teachers at Ashland Junior High school in the afternoon.

"Specifically, he urged the teaching personnel to prepare today's generation for going out into space by teaching them to keep an open mind, submerge their egos and increase their scope of reality.

" 'The human ego is the greatest obstacle to human learning,' Fry remarked. 'Up to now we've stayed in our own back yard, and we've been able to beat ourselves on the chests and think how important we are. But now we are getting ready to go out into other people's back yards, and we had better prepare for it.

" 'We once thought we were the center of the universe,' he explained. 'Then our ego took a blow when we discovered that the earth merely revolves around the sun.

" 'Then our ego took another blow when we found that the sun is merely an insignificant star in a galaxy that has around 100 billion stars. And still another blow when we found that our galaxy is merely one of many galaxies, at least 10 billion of them known today.

" 'The human race at that point still took comfort in believing that it was unique in the universe, but then astronomers began to assume that planets are a common occurrence throughout creation,' Fry said.

"Referring to the Harvard astronomer's statistics on extra-terrestrial life, he said the most pessimistic estimates are that only one star out of 10 has planets, but that each solar system has an average of 10 planets. Therefore, if we assume there are 10 billion stars in our galaxy, then there are about 100 billion planets,' he explained.

"Next he said, 'The most pessimistic estimates concerning which planets have conditions for life are one in 100, which would leave one billion planets in the galaxy with such conditions."

"Then he asked the audiences to assume that only one out of every 10 planets with suitable conditions had actually developed life, which would still leave 100 million with life.

"Finally, assuming that only one out of 100 of these had passed the earth's present level of development, there would be one million planets with space craft engaged in travel.

" 'Life develops in the center of a galaxy first, and earth is located on the outer reaches of its galaxy,' he said, explaining why he thought numerous civilizations in the Milky Way had achieved space travel as many as two million years ago.

"One member of the audience at Ashland asked Fry how beings would traverse the immense distances in space, to which he replied that he thought there was no limit to the speed with which men can learn to travel.

" 'The theory of relativity does not say that man cannot travel faster than the speed of light,' he remarked. 'It merely says that no one on earth will be able to see him do it. (See chapter 4, page 44 for an explanation of this.)

"In other portions of his talks, Fry called the rocket concept outmoded and compared it to propelling a rowboat across a lake by thrusting an oar out the rear. No intelligent man would use such a method if he were aware of other possibilities.'

"Referring to 'other possibilities' in regard to space travel, he predicted that the United States will within eight years develop space craft that use the more efficient gravitational field mechanism method of propulsion. These craft will literally fall off the earth by reversing the path of gravity that hold everything to earth, he predicted.

"He said the only reason such craft have not been developed before is that earth men have only recently come to realize that such propulsion is possible.

" 'Throughout history, man's stumbling block has been his refusal to recognize that something is possible,' Fry said. 'Once he recognizes that something is possible, it isn't long before he actually does it.'

"Recognizing that things are possible was one of the points Fry appeared to be getting at when he urged teachers to enlarge the scope of their student's scope of reality.

" 'Reality has no boundaries,' he said. 'It is not small nor limited—it is infinite. People draw a circle around what they consider to be real, but all that circle shows is the level of consciousness they have reached.' "

A few days after the above article was published, a columnist added these comments:

"There were a number of interesting points that we were unable to squeeze into last week's story of the talks that Daniel W. Fry gave for the teachers of the Medford and Ashland districts.

"The news story led off with Fry's prediction that there are students in high school today who will walk on the surface of Mars and Venus before they are 30, but we didn't have 'space' to go through the somewhat complicated explanation of how he arrived at this prediction.

"Fry stated that present-day scientific development is traveling upward on a rapidly rising curve. He calls it 'The Curve of Development.'

" 'Developments,' he said, 'made during the past 10 years equal those made in the previous 100 and those made in the previous 100 equaled what was accomplished in the preceding 1,000 years, and so forth.

" 'Some anthropologists estimate it took one million years for man to progress from the stone ax to the bow and arrow,' he said. 'An engineer today could do it in 30 minutes, or in an afternoon at the most.'

"Applying this 'curve of development' theory to the subject of landing men on Mars and Venus, he looks at it in this way; 'Ten years ago we thought we could do it in about 200 years. Eight years ago we thought we might do it in 100. Five years ago the estimate dropped to around 50. And so on.'

"That is why Fry thinks earth man will land on Mars and Venus in about 10 years.

" 'The Saturn rocket which has the thrust to reach Mars and Venus has been tested with results that exceeded expectations,' he said. 'And we have put men into orbit. If we had less concern for the safety of our astronauts, we might be able to put one on Mars or Venus within one year.'

"Looking at scientific development in general, he made the remark that when Jules Verne wrote his science-fiction books, he was writing to the limit of the imagination of that era. 'Just about everything that Jules Verne imagined has come to pass, so extrapolating the same situation upward on the curve of development, we can predict that everything within man's imagination today will become reality within perhaps as little as 20 years.'

"That's quite a statement, but he holds to it.

8

"This curve of development theory which Fry expounds so well is one explanation Fry gives when people ask him how man can possibly hope to travel to planets and star systems that are hundreds, thousands, and millions of light years away from earth. He sees no reason why man cannot learn to travel at tremendous speeds well in excess of the speed of light.

"At one time, earthlings believed that no man could travel as fast as 60 miles per hour without being crushed by the atmospheric pressure, he points out. Barney Oldfield proved them wrong when he was the first man to drive 60 miles per hour in an automobile. Today, astronauts go 18,000 miles per hour when in orbit."

In sincere appreciation of your interest in the subject of U. F. O.'s, I want to thank you for buying and reading this book.

DANIEL W. FRY, Ph.D.

I

I See and Touch
a Flying Saucer

Tonight, July 4, 1950, I joined an ever growing group of individuals around the world who are known as "U. F. O. observers" or "Saucer Sighters."

Not only have I seen one, I have touched it, entered it, and even made a short test hop as a passenger.

Also, I have communicated at some length with its operator.

Now that this unusual vehicle has gone, I am back in my quarters at the White Sands Proving Ground near Las Cruces, New Mexico.

To many who read this book it may seem incredible that such an event could really have happened. But it did.

It would not be easy to explain. In fact, I have often asked myself, "Why, with more than two billion people who inhabit this planet, should fate have chosen me to be the beneficiary of this unique and interesting event?

"The mathematical improbability of its occurrence is so great that the moment I tried to convince someone else I have ridden in a 'flying saucer' and conversed with a being from 'somewhere in space,' they might suggest I be sent to the nearest asylum."

Still, this is the greatest and most exciting event in my life, and I can't keep it entirely to myself. So I have decided to write a detailed account of the event, exactly as it happened while it is still sharp and clear in my memory.

*   *   *

Since this was the Fourth of July, I planned to go into Las Cruces with the other scientists and engineers at the White Sands Proving Grounds, do a little mild celebrating and see the display of fireworks which was scheduled for that evening.

Most of the Aerojet group with whom I worked had left for Las Cruces in the company car during the afternoon. Since the car was crowded, I decided to wait and take a bus later in the day. I misunderstood the departure time, however, missed the last bus and found myself stranded in an almost deserted camp with nothing much to do except sit in my room and read.

I began with a textbook by James Cork on the subject of "Heat Transfer." The subject proved to be quite appropriate to the circumstances because, by eight-thirty, it was unbearably hot and stuffy in my room and I decided to take a walk in the hope that it would be cooler outside.

I headed first in the direction of the old V2 static test stand on which we were mounting our large rocket motor for testing. The stand is about a mile and a half from the cluster of buildings which form the nucleus of the proving ground and the distance was just right for a leisurely hike in the relative coolness of the evening air.

About two-thirds of the way to the test stand, a small dirt road intersects the main road and leads off to the right toward the base of the Organ mountains. When I reached this point I suddenly decided to take the dirt road instead of continuing out toward the test stand.

The road was hardly more than a pair of wheel tracks in the desert and they wound in and out among the dunes. It was less than two miles long, but it was the only road in the area which I had never been on, and I decided that so long as exercise and pastime were the only goals of the hike, this road would serve as well as any.

The sun had been down for nearly an hour and there was little daylight left, but in the clear air of this high desert region, there is always plenty of light for a comfortable hike at any time of the night unless the sky is overcast.

13

As I scanned the sky, my eyes rested on a group of especially bright stars just over the peaks of the mountains. Suddenly one of the stars went out. This immediately riveted my attention on that spot, for stars don't just go out, at least not in a cloudless sky. Something was eclipsing the star, but I had no idea what it could be.

An airplane would require less than a second to pass a given spot, and the star did not come back into sight. Also, in the silence of the desert at night, a plane could be heard much farther than it could be seen, and there was no sound at all.

No weather balloons were released at night, and in any event, a weather balloon would rise quite rapidly and would, therefore, only eclipse a star for a few seconds.

Then another star just to the right of the first went out, and a few seconds later two more just below.

A strong prickling sensation traveled up my spine. Whatever it was that was cutting off the light of the stars was increasing rapidly in apparent diameter, and since the bearing remained constant it could only mean that the object was coming directly toward me.

Finally I could see what it was. At the same time, I realized why I had not been able to see it sooner. Its color appeared to be nearly identical to the color of the night sky so that, even when it was quite close, it was difficult to make out anything but the outline.

14

As it continued to come toward me, I felt a strong inclination to run. But long experience in blasting and rocket work had taught me that it is foolish to run from an approaching object until you are sure of its trajectory because there is no way to judge the trajectory of a missile if you are running.

The object was now less than a few hundred feet away. It began to move more slowly, not more than ten to fifteen miles per hour and seemed to decelerate at a pace that would bring it slowly to a stop before it reached the ground. I could also see that its shape was an oblate spheroid about thirty feet in diameter at the equator or largest part.

Somewhat reassured by its slowness of motion, I remained where I was and watched it glide in as lightly as a bit of thistle floating down in the breeze. About seventy feet away it settled to the ground without the slightest bump or jar.

Except for the crackling of the brush beneath it, it made no sound. For nearly a minute I stood motionless. A ghostly feeling crept over me and I stared at the object as mystified and spellbound as a child might be observing some new and unusual performance at a circus.

During the many years I have been employed in the field of aircraft and spacecraft design, I have helped to develop many guided missiles. Through my work at the White Sands Proving Grounds and other such

15

centers of development, I had become well acquainted with most of the recent advances in aeronautics. But here was a device so far advanced over anything I had ever heard of that I felt like the backwoods farmer who saw his first giraffe and said, "I see it, but I don't believe it."

My first conscious thought was, "This unusual craft might be something secretly developed by the Soviet Union."

We knew that the Russians claimed to be ahead of us in the development of large rockets, but this was obviously not a rocket.

I reflected a moment, then became convinced that this could not be a device created in the Soviet Union, or anywhere else on earth. The intelligence and the technology that had designed and built this craft had found the answer to a number of questions which our best physicists had not yet learned to ask.

The ship's operation was silent. No propellors churned the air. I saw no flash and roar of incandescent gas was hurled from nozzles to produce thrust. The ship simply coasted in quietly and settled gently to earth.

Before landing, it had slowed to only a few miles per hour, yet it showed no sign of falling. Only a heliocopter or a "lighter than air" craft could duplicate this feat. But there were no propellers on this vehicle. And the fact that the brush was crushed flat

16

under it when it settled to the ground, proved conclusively that this was no "lighter than air craft."

Whatever this vehicle might be, it could certainly operate efficiently and effortlessly in violation of the law of gravity.

While all the above was going through my mind, I slowly approached the ship. My instinct and reason, however, told me I should put as much distance as possible between myself and this unknown, and unpredictable device.

Like most of the scientists engaged in the field of research, I have been endowed since birth with an eager and active curiosity. When the object of that curiosity is of a scientific nature, especially when it seemed to be an important advance in technology, the curiosity becomes a driving force which sweeps all reason before it.

I approached within a few feet of the craft and paused to watch and listen for any sign of life or sound which might come from within. There was neither.

While the ship stood silent and motionless on the desert sand, I circled it slowly and examined it carefully. It was as if it had appeared from the air, a spheroid, considerably flattened at the top and bottom. The vertical dimension was about sixteen feet, and the horizontal diameter was about thirty feet at the widest point, which was about seven feet above the ground.

Its curvature was such that when viewed from below, at an angle of less than 45 degrees from the vertical, it appeared to be saucer-shaped, although it was actually shaped more like a soup bowl inverted over a sauce dish.

The dark blue color which at first it appeared to be was now gone. A closer inspection showed that the highly polished metal surface was silvery in color, with a slight violet iridescence. I walked completely around the craft without seeing any sign of opening or seams. "If there is anyone inside," I thought, "they must get in through the top or bottom."

I paused then, to more carefully appraise the situation.

What should I do next? Should I return to the base and report the advent of this strange new craft?

At first, this seemed the logical thing to do, but then another thought intervened. It would take at least three quarters of an hour for me to get back to the base, find someone in authority, and return with other observers.

What if the craft took off in the meantime? There would be nothing but a crumpled patch of brush to substantiate my story. Who would believe me? If anyone did believe me, who would readily admit it?

I had read of the ridicule heaped upon those who had stated they had seen some unexplained objects flying in the air. How much worse would I be criticized if I claimed to have seen one land and been close enough to touch it, yet had no proof of the fact except a flattened patch of brush.

Then I realized that, although I had been close enough to touch the craft for several minutes, I had not, as yet, actually done so. Perhaps I could learn something about the material of which it was made, by the feel. At any rate I could tell the temperature.

I stepped forward and carefully touched the polished metal. It was only a few degrees above the air temperature and incredibly smooth.

It is difficult to describe the degree of smoothness. If you were to run your finger over a large pearl which had been covered with a thin soap film you might receive a sensation somewhat similar to that which I felt when I touched the metal of this ship. I stroked the ship with the palm of my hand and felt a slight but definite tingling in the tips of my fingers and the heel of my palm.

Then a crisp voice came out of the air at my side, "Better not touch the hull, pal, it's still hot!"

I had not realized how much tension I was under until the voice suddenly shattered the silence. I leaped backwards several feet, caught my heel in a low bush and sprawled at full length in the sand. I heard something that sounded like a low chuckle, then the voice came again in a somewhat friendlier tone, "Take it easy, pal, you're among friends."

The humiliation of my ungraceful posture, combined with the mild tone of the voice and its familiar phrases, served to sweep away the fear I felt and replaced it with a mild irritation. I arose, brushed off my clothes, and tugged at a sand burr which had found a home in my hair.

I looked for some person or gadget from which the voice might come, but could find none. "You could have turned the volume down," I grumbled. "You didn't have to blast out at me like that. You scared me out of a week's growth."

"Blast out?" the voice hesitated. "Oh yes, you mean the amplitude of the warning was too great. Sorry, but you were about to kill yourself and there wasn't time to diddle with controls."

"Do you mean that the hull is highly radioactive?" I asked. "If so, I am still much too close."

"It isn't radioactive," was the reply. "I used the term 'hot' because it was the best I could think of in your language to explain the condition. The hull has a field about it which repels all other matter. Your physicists would describe the force involved as the 'anti' aspect of the binding energy of the atom.

"When certain elements such as platinum are properly prepared and treated with a saturation exposure to a beam of very high energy photons, the binding energy particle will be generated outside the nucleus. Since these particles tend to repel each other as well as all matter they, like the electron, tend to migrate to the surface of the metal where they manifest as a repellent force.

"The particles have a life of several weeks of your time, so that the normal cosmic radiation received by the craft when in space is sufficient to maintain an effective charge. The field is very powerful at molecular distances but dimishes by the seventh power of the distance so that the force becomes negligible a few microns away from the hull.

"Perhaps you noticed that the surface seemed smooth and slippery. That is because your flesh did not actually touch the metal but was held a short distance from the surface by the repulsion of the field. We use the field to protect the hull from being scratched or damaged in landing. It also lowers air friction tremendously when it is necessary to travel at high speed through an atmosphere."

"But how would this kill me?" I asked. "I did touch the hull and felt only a slight tingle in my hand. And what did you mean, by that remark about *my* language? If you aren't an American then I never heard one myself."

"As to your first question," the voice replied, "it wouldn't have killed you at once. In fact, it might have taken several months, but it would have been just as certain as if it had been instantaneous.

"The best way that I can explain it to you is to say that exposure of the human skin to the force field which is present around the ship causes the skin to produce what you earth people call 'antibodies' in the blood stream. For some reason which we don't yet fully understand, these antibodies are absorbed by the liver, whose function they attack causing the liver to become greatly enlarged and congested.

"In cases where the skin is exposed to the field for a minute or more death is practically certain. In your case, I don't think you have been exposed long enough to be in any great danger; although you will undoubtedly feel some effects sooner or later, provided, of course, that your biological functions are identical with ours and we have every reason to believe that they are.

"As to your second question, I am not an American such as you, although my present assignment requires me to become one. The fact that you believed me to be one of your countrymen is a testimonial to the success of the effort I have expended during the last two of your years, to learn and practice the use of your language and idiom.

"As a matter of fact, I have never yet set foot upon your planet. It will require at least four more of your years for me to become adapted to your atmosphere and gravity and to become immunized to your biotics."

I stood silently for what seemed like a long time and

attempted to digest the full meaning and implication of his words.

At last I said slowly, "If my own eyes had not seen this craft come in and land, I might have concluded I had been reading too many 'science fiction' stories. But my scientific training and years of study about space prepared me to admit the possibility of almost anything. Besides, since my being here and seeing you land is entirely accidental, it is obvious that my belief or disbelief could not be of the slightest importance to you."

"On the contrary," replied the voice. "It is important to us that you be given every opportunity to acquaint yourself with the facts and to form your own opinion accordingly.

"One of the principal purposes of this expedition is to determine the basic adaptability of those who inhabit the earth, particularly your ability to adapt your minds quickly and calmly to conceptions which are completely foreign to your customary modes of thought.

"Previous expeditions by our ancestors over a period of many centuries met with almost total failure in this respect. This time there is hope that we may be able to find minds which are better trained and more receptive so that we may assist you in the progress of your race.

"In your own case, your conduct has pleased me and surpassed our best expectations."

"I can see," I said, "that your race, whatever it is, and ours has at least one thing in common; that sarcasm is the principal form of humor. However, you can't annoy me that way. I've been kidded by experts.

"I realize that everything I have done since you first came into sight has been wrong. In the first place, if I had any sense, I would have gotten out of here fast when I first saw you coming, instead of waiting, perhaps to be crushed under the ship.

"When you landed, instead of leaving, or at least remaining at a comparatively safe distance, I had to come snooping around your craft. Then, when your warning voice came through your speaker—or whatever it is—instead of accepting the warning calmly and quickly, I jumped like a scared rabbit and landed in the sand in as undignified a position as it is possible to imagine.

"Last, but not least, you apparently suppose that I believe the statements which you have made. As I said before, I am prepared to consider the possibility that they are true. I am also prepared to consider the possibility that they are not true."

"Precisely," replied the voice. "Let me explain my position. No sarcasm was intended. I meant exactly what I said. In the first place you said that curiosity impelled you to investigate the craft, subjecting your-self to unknown hazards rather than to seek safety in flight.

"This typifies the struggle between the desire for knowledge and the desire for the safety of the status quo.

"I believe there is an old saying among your people that self-preservation is the first law of nature. It is encouraging to note that your desire for knowledge can occasionally overcome a basic animal instinct.

"When I called a warning to you, your reaction was not one of fear as you seem to think. A true reaction of fear would have frozen you into immobility at least for a moment. Instead, you acted instantly and in the proper manner.

"The fact is, that in spite of being in circumstances completely unique in your experience, you are listen-ing calmly to my voice and making logical replies. This is the best evidence that your mind is of the type we hoped to find."

"Thank you for the compliments," I said. "I would like to believe I deserve them, but your statement implies that you propose to use me in some project which involves the scientific advancement of the people now living on this earth.

"Why me? Just because I accidently happened to be here when you landed? I could easily put you in touch with several reliable men right here at the rocket-testing base who are considered to be more advanced in science than I."

"When you say that you happen to be here by the merest accident, you underestimate our ability to select the ones to whom we wish to speak," was the reply.

"The brains of many earth men transmit readily, but you are one of those rare individuals whose brain also receives well.

"We have carefully investigated the minds of many of your top scientists. In every case we found that their minds had hardened into a mould based on their present conceptions. Their minds have advanced to an extent where they believe they know almost everything in the scientific world. So they find it difficult to change their minds or form new opinions.

"I can make my meaning clearer by an analogy. A man who seeks scientific knowledge is like an ant climbing a tree. He knows when he is moving upward but his vision is short and he is unable to encompass the entire trunk. The result is, he may get out on a lower limb without realizing he has left the main trunk.

"All goes well for a time. He can still climb upward and pluck a few of the fruits of his progress, but soon he begins to become confused as the solid branch which he first considered to be the trunk, suddenly begins to break up into myriads of twigs and leaves all pointing in different directions.

26

"So the seeker of knowledge finds that the great 'basic laws,' which he once thought were unshakable, now begin to divide and to point in opposite directions.

"As a result of this seeming confusion, the scientist comes to the conclusion that he is approaching the limit of the knowledge which can be conceived and that all physical laws ultimately become purely statistical.

"When he reaches this point, the only way he can make further progress is to follow a line of abstract mathematical reasoning.

"It is like traveling on a train in one of your subways. Eventually you may arrive at your destination, yet you cannot see where you are going. So you have no way of knowing whether you could have chosen a much shorter and easier way to get to the same place.

"Your science is now in such a position.

"For example, your scientists now feel obligated to state that the electron is at the same time both a particle and a wave motion. They attempt to rationalize this by saying that the electron is a particle in a wave of probability. This is a condition which cannot be visualized by the mind and the only means of progress they can find are through the subways of abstract mathematics.

"You will find that fundamental truths are always simple and understandable when they are viewed from the proper perspective. So the branch of knowledge

27

your people have developed is understandable as a 'branch' when it is viewed from above while looking down the main trunk.

"In short, what your science must do if it is to continue to progress, is to go back down the limb on which you are trapped to the point where it joins the main trunk and then start up again.

"This we can and will help your people to do, but only if they wish it and are able to follow the path which we will point out. It will be given to you sometime in the future.

"Before we can be of assistance to you people on earth, two things must be accomplished. First, our bodies must become adapted, biologically, to your environment so that when we come among you we will be identical with your people. This, as I said before, will require at least four more years.

"The second is more difficult.

"The political tensions which now exist between the many nations of Earth must be eased. If any one of the nations that dominate one or more others on your planet were to achieve conclusive scientific superiority over the other, then under present conditions, a war of extermination would likely follow.

"We are not here to assist any nation to make war but to stimulate a degree of progress which will eliminate the reasons for wars on earth, even as we, some thousands of years ago have eliminated the reasons for conflict and misunderstanding among our own people.

28

2

I Take a Ride
in the Flying Saucer

I SEE you are becoming weary standing out there in the sand listening to these dissertations on science and sociology.

"Which reminds me of my duties as a host. Would you like to enter the ship and perhaps make a short flight? It is only a cargo carrier with remote control, but it does have a small passenger compartment with several seats which are plain but quite comfortable."

"I would certainly like to see the inside of your ship," I replied. "And I would give anything to be allowed to ride in it, but how can I get in?

"I have been completely around the ship and saw no sign of any opening. Also you said you are not yet accustomed to our atmosphere. If I come in I will have to bring my atmosphere with me. How will that affect you?"

"As I said before," replied the voice, "the craft is a

29

remotely controlled cargo carrier. I am not in this craft. I am in the central unit, or what you would call the 'mother ship.' At present it is some nine hundred miles above the surface of your planet.

"This cargo craft is being used to bring us samples of your atmosphere so that we can accustom ourselves to it. The cargo hold is evacuated so that when I open the intake port, the hold becomes filled with the atmosphere of your planet and takes it in at whatever temperature and pressure exists there.

"Also any bacteria which are in the air are brought along for study and for the production of the anti-toxins we need to withstand any diseases you have.

"The intake port is on the top of the craft. I will open it now."

An unusual sound broke the stillness of the night. It was partly a hiss and partly a murmur. It lasted for about fifteen seconds and came from the top of the ship. I was surprised at the small volume of the sound. Any port large enough to have filled a ship that size with air in fifteen seconds should have produced quite a roar. Then I realized that the hull was almost, if not entirely, sound-proof and since most of the sound of the entering air would have been produced inside the hull, very little would be audible outside.

Then I heard a single click come from the surface of the ship, a small but sharp click such as might have come from the operation of a single arm relay or a small solenoid, and a portion of the bottom of the hull

30

ACTUAL PHOTOGRAPH FROM COLOR MOVIES TAKEN BY DANIEL FRY, PH.D.

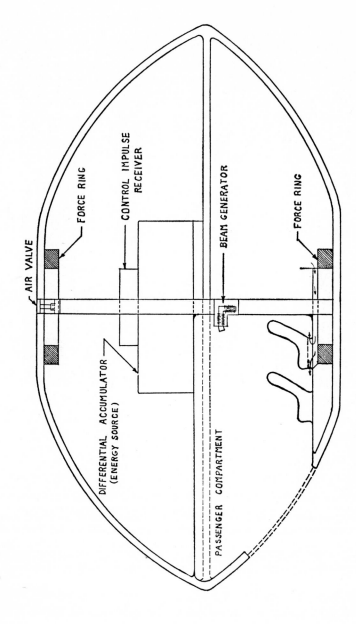

INSIDE OF SPACE SHIP DESCRIBED BY DANIEL FRY, PH.D.

just to my left moved back upon itself for a distance of several inches and then moved sideways, disappearing into the wall of the hull, leaving an oval-shaped opening about five feet in height and three feet wide. I moved over to the port or hatch, whichever it might be called, ducked my head slightly and advanced into the opening. Because of the curvature of the hull, of course, my head was inside the craft while my feet were still on the ground.

The compartment into which I was looking occupied only a small portion of the interior of the ship. It was a room about nine feet deep and seven feet wide, with the floor about sixteen inches above the ground and the ceiling slightly over six feet above the floor.

The walls were slightly curved and the intersections of the walls were bevelled so that there were no sharp angles or corners. Of course, the wall nearest me, through which the opening led, was the hull itself and had the same curvature inside and out. This wall was about four inches thick and it was the wall into which the door or hatch had been drawn.

The room contained four seats. They looked much like our modern body contour chairs except they were somewhat smaller than the ones to which we are accustomed. The seats faced the opening in which I was standing and were arranged in two rows of two each in the center of the room. This left an aisle between the seats and either wall.

In the center of the rear wall, where it joined the

31

ceiling, there was a box or cabinet with a tube and lens which resembled a small motion picture projector, except no visible film spools or any other moving parts were visible. Light was coming from this lens. It was not a beam of light such as would come from a motion picture projector but a diffused glow. While it did not seem especially bright, it still furnished enough light for comfortable seeing.

The seats and the light seemed to be the only furnishings in the otherwise bare metal room. "Not a very inviting cabin," I thought, "looks more like a cell."

"As I said before; it's plain, but you'll find the seat comfortable," said the voice. "Step in and take a seat if you wish to ride. We don't have too much time."

Almost automatically I stepped up and on to the floor of the cabin then started for one of the seats. Before I reached it, I heard a click as the door began to slide out of its recess in the wall behind me. Instinctively, I half turned as though to leap out to the comparative safety of the open desert behind me, but the door was already closed. If this was a trap, I was in it and there was no use now to struggle against the inevitable.

"Where would you like to go?" came the voice again. This time it did not seem to be coming from beside me but rather from all around me, as though I were hearing words which I myself was speaking.

32

"I don't know how far you can take me in the time you have," I replied. "And since this compartment has no windows, it won't matter which way we go, as I won't be able to see anything."

"You will be able to see," was the reply. "At least as much as you could see from any vehicle in the air at night. If you would like a suggestion we can take you over New York City and return you here in about thirty minutes. The light pattern of New York City at night from about twenty miles up has always been to us one of the most impressive sights to be seen on your planet."

"To New York—and back—in thirty minutes!" I said. "That's eight thousand miles per hour! How can you produce energies of that order on a craft like this, and how can I stand the acceleration? You don't even have seat belts on these seats!"

"You won't feel any ill effects from the acceleration," was the reply. "In fact, you won't feel the acceleration at all. Just take a seat, and I will start the craft. I will explain some of the things which puzzle you, during the ride."

I sat down in the left front seat which was the one nearest the door and found that it was indeed very comfortable. The material of which it was made felt like foam rubber with vinylite covering. However, there were no seams or joints such as an outer covering would require, so the material, whatever it was, probably had been moulded into its frame in a single operation.

Then the voice broke into my thoughts again. "I will now turn off the compartment light and turn on the viewing beam."

For a moment the room became utterly dark. Then the projector again became active. This time it was not a diffused glow, but a beam—just as in a movie or slide projector. The beam, or that part of it which was visible at all, was a deep violet, at the very top of the visible spectrum. The beam spread over the door, through which I had come, and the door disappeared. It did not slide back into the wall as it had before. It simply ceased to exist, at least visually. It was as though I were looking through the finest type of plate glass or lucite window.

"There isn't time to give you a complete understanding of all the things which you would like to know about this craft and about us, but perhaps I can explain a few of the basic principles about which you seem to be curious," the voice said.

I was just beginning to realize that the words which I had been hearing were not coming to my ears as sound waves at all but rather were originating directly in my brain.

"As you see," the voice continued, "the door has become transparent. This startles you, because you are accustomed to thinking of metals being completely opaque. However, ordinary glass is just as dense as many metals and harder than most and yet transmits light quite readily.

"Most matter is opaque to light because the photons of light are captured and absorbed in the electron orbits of the atoms through which they pass. This capture will occur whenever the frequency of the photon matches one of the frequencies of the atom. The energy thus stored is then re-emitted, but usually in the infra-red portion of the spectrum, which is below the range of visibility, and so cannot be seen as light.

"There are several ways in which almost any matter can be made transparent, or at least translucent.

"One method is to create a field matrix between the atoms which will tend to prevent the photon from being absorbed. Such a matrix develops in many substances during crystallization.

"Another is to raise the frequency of the photon above the highest absorbtion frequency of the atoms. The beam of energy, which is now acting on the metal of the door, is what you would call a frequency multiplier. The beam penetrates the metal and acts upon any light that reaches it in such a way that the frequency of the light is multiplied to that of the range between what you know as the 'X-ray' and the 'Cosmic Ray' spectrums.

"At these frequencies, the waves pass through the metal quite readily. Then, when these leave the metal

35

on the inside of the door, they again interact with the viewing beam, producing what you would call beat frequencies which are identical with the original frequencies of the light.

"As a rough analogy the system could be compared to the carrier wave of one of your radio broadcasting stations, and the modulation is applied 'upstream' as it were, instead of at the source of the carrier.

"If you are ready I will now start the craft."

Instinctively, I braced myself in the seat and gripped the sides with my hands. A moment later, the ground suddenly fell away from the ship with incredible rapidity.

I say that the ground "fell away" because I did not feel the slightest sense of motion myself, and the ship was as steady as a rock. In spite of the fact that we must have been accelerating at the rate of at least ten g's, I felt no strain on my body and it seemed we were standing still.

The lights of the army base at the proving ground, which had been hidden by a small hill, sprang into sight instantly and began drawing together like a flock of baby chicks when called by the mother hen. A few seconds later the lights of the town of Las Cruces came into view in the lower left hand corner of the window, and I knew that we had risen at least a thousand feet in those two or three seconds. The ship was rotating slightly to my left as it rose, and I was also able to see the highway from Las Cruces to El Paso, a narrow but brillant ribbon illuminated by the headlights of the many cars that were upon it.

The lights of El Paso and Ciudad Juarez, Mexico, gave out a solid glow on the horizon, but as we continued to rise, they broke up into patches of varied brilliancy. I could see the hundreds of lights of Fort Bliss, the patch which represented the Presidio area and the intensely bright spot which was downtown El Paso.

I could even distinguish the thin dark line of the Rio Grande River which separated El Paso from its Mexican twin, Ciudad Juarez. A few seconds later the ship rotated until the lights of those cities passed out of view.

The viewing screen was now pointed southeast and had stopped revolving. The surface of the earth appeared to be glowing with a slightly greenish phosphorescence. At the same time, the sky outside of the ship became much darker, and the stars seemed to have doubled in brilliance.

"We must have entered the stratosphere," I thought. "If so, we must have risen more than ten miles in what can't have been more than fifteen or twenty seconds, yet I have not felt the slightest sensation of acceleration."

"You are now about thirteen miles above the earth's surface," I heard the voice say. "And you are rising at approximately one-half mile per second. We have brought you up rather slowly so that you could have a better opportunity to view your local cities from the air. We will take you up to thirty-five miles for the horizontal flight. At that level the residual atmosphere is attenuated to a degree which offers no appreciable resistance to the motion of the craft."

"By the way," I said, "What happened to the moon? It must be somewhere in the sky, but everything looks so dark outside."

"It looks dark," was the reply, "simply because there is not sufficient atmosphere at this level to diffuse the light. You would not see any evidence of the moonlight unless it were shining directly on the viewing screen. I have purposely kept the craft from rotating far enough for this to happen, as the light is quite intense above the atmosphere, and it would be difficult, if not impossible, to see anything else while it was visible.

"Now that you are high enough, I can begin to add a substantial horizontal component to your vertical motion.

"Since there will be little of interest to see during the next few minutes I will take this time to explain a few of the things that puzzle you. In the first place; you mentioned something about 'seat belts' and questioned whether you could endure the acceleration. This is a question which seems to have come up quite frequently in the minds of the men of science on your planet.

"Whenever our vehicles have been observed by any of your people, and when the velocities and accelerations of these craft are described, disbelief is always apparent. We have heard that some of your most learned men have made the statement that: 'No human being or other higher form of life, as we know it, could survive acceleration of this order.' This has always been a matter of disappointment to us in our evaluation of the intelligence of the people of earth.

"It seems to us that even a moderately intelligent layman with the average knowledge which you people possess should be able to refute this statement at once.

"The answer is simply that the force which accelerates the vehicle is identical in nature to a gravitational field. It not only acts upon every atom of the vehicle itself but also acts equally upon every atom of mass which is within it, including the pilot or passengers.

"In your airplane the situation is entirely different. You have propellers or jets, which produce a thrust upon one part of the ship. This local thrust accelerates the ship but not the pilot. The pilot is accelerated only by thrust against those parts of his body which are in contact with the seats upon which he sits. Because of the inertia of the remainder of the body, compression is produced which causes the feeling of acceleration, or in extreme cases, blackout or actual crushing of the body. Our only limit of acceleration is the limit of available force."

"But in this case," I thought, "why am I not floating

39

around in the air as things are supposed to do within a missile which is in free fall?"

"The answer to this also should be fairly obvious," was the reply. "Before the ship was put into motion, you were resting upon the seat, and there was force of one gravity acting between your body and the seat. Since the force which accelerates both the ship and your body acts in exact proportion to the mass, and since the earth's gravity continues to act upon both, the original force between your body and the seat will remain constant, except that it will decrease as the force of gravity of the planet decreases with distance.

"When traveling between planetary bodies, far from any source of natural gravity, we find it necessary, for practical reasons, to reproduce this force artificially.

"The gravity to which we are accustomed is but little more than one-half of that which exists upon the earth. This is the principal reason that it will take so much time for us to become ordinary members of your race.

"If we were to land now upon the surface of your planet and leave the protection of our ships, the high gravitational force would put a severe strain upon our internal organs, which in a few days would produce serious illness, and eventually death.

"This is not merely calculation. We know it to be true because it has been tried several times in the past. By remaining in our ships where we can control the force to which we are subjected, and by increasing that force by small but regular increments, we can build up the supporting tissues and strengthen our muscular systems until, eventually, your gravity will become as natural to use as our own is now.

"When this time comes, it is our hope that you and a few other members of your race, who have been willing to retain an open mind, will be able to assist us in bridging the considerable gulf which exists between our culture and yours. As I explained before, we will never attempt to force either our knowledge or our culture upon you and will never come to your people unless there is substantial evidence that they desire it, and there is certainly no such evidence at the present time!

"It is true that the purpose of the expedition is not entirely philanthropic. There are some materials upon your planet which we could use to the advantage of both our peoples, material which you have in great abundance but which are rather scarce elsewhere in this solar system. While we desire the use of these materials, our service to you people will not be made contingent upon such use. Any knowledge or assistance which we can give will be freely offered."

"Could you explain to me the principles of operation of this craft?" I asked. "How do you produce the tremendous amounts of energy necessary to accelerate a ship like this to such high velocities, and how do you apply that energy without producing any outward evidence of its application?"

"In order to do this," was the reply, "I would have

to give you an entirely new groundwork in Basic Physics. Your science attempts to make one of the lower limbs take the place of the entire tree of knowledge. As a result your scientific knowledge remains limited and, in many ways, overcomplicated. Then, when scientists attempt to apply this limited knowledge to practical ends, the result is an apparatus which is unwieldy and, oftentimes, complex.

"For example, certain engineers and scientists of your country are now engaged in planning a submarine to be driven by what you call atomic or nuclear energy. They plan to do this by constructing a 'pile' in which the lighter isotope of uranium (235) fissions producing heat energy and free neutrons which are absorbed by the heavier isotope or uranium (238) converting it into the next heavier element in the transuranic series which also, in turn, is fissionable. (Pu-239)

"While that method is rather complicated, it is still the most potent source of energy differential which your people have yet produced, but in order to convert this heat energy into propulsion of the ship, they plan to circulate a working fluid through the 'pile' to absorb the heat; circulate the 'working fluid' through a heat exchanger to convert another fluid to vapor under pressure, pass the vapor through a turbine to produce torque and, finally, use the turbine to drive a generator to produce an electrical current.

"If they achieve an overall efficiency of thirty percent it will be a great feat of engineering because it is based on your present limited knowledge.

"If your scientists and engineers were capable of thinking in simpler terms they could, with but little advance in the knowledge they now possess, construct a simple thermopile about the fission pile and convert the resulting temperature gradient directly into electric energy with an efficiency of at least ninety to ninety-four per cent, with no moving parts, at a smaller cost, and considerably less mass per unit of energy output."

"Compared with our methods, even this system would seem wastefully complex."

"Your greatest need is to discover the utter simplicity of the basic laws or facts of nature. Then you will easily be able to produce effects which now seem to you to be impossible."

3

The Inside of the Ship
Is Explained to Me

I SHOULD like very much to learn more about the interior of this ship and how it operates," I said. "If the details of your mother craft are too difficult as a starter, how about trying me out on the details of the one I am in?

"If I close my eyes and concentrate, won't it be possible for you to give me at least a cross-sectional view of this ship?"

"Hardly," Alan replied a little dryly. "You are making the error which your people so often make when they attempt to define what you call 'extra-sensory perception.'

"In the first place, it isn't 'extra-sensory' at all. It is just as much a part of the normal perception equipment of your body as any of your other five senses. It has been used so little by your people that it is under-developed and exists only in a rudimentary state.

Some of your animals, however, and many of your insects have developed this sense to a higher degree than your people.

"You have been accustomed from birth to receive and resolve all of your visual impressions with your eyes wide open. You will remember that when you first learned to use a microscope, you were taught that even though there was only one eyepiece, it was best to keep both eyes open. Therefore, do not close your eyes. I will turn off the viewing beam so that there will be no distracting influence.

"Secondly, do not concentrate. Concentration is the attitude of transmission and is almost a complete bar to reception. To receive impressions easily and properly, you must achieve a state of complete relaxation. This you have the ability to do, and it is an ability which is remarkable in one of your race.

"In fact it was through this ability that I first made contact with your mind. It was three nights ago. You had returned to your bed but you found it difficult to sleep because the pressure of the events of the day had been unusually great. You made use of a mental device which was very interesting to me because of its simplicity and effectiveness. Do you remember what it was?"

"Oh yes," I said. "I use it often when sleep doesn't come readily. I simply visualize a room which is completely dark except for ten luminous numerals on the far wall of the room. I focus my attention upon these numerals until all other thoughts have been excluded from my consciousness. I then begin, one by one to erase the numerals, keeping my mind focused upon the remaining ones, but lowering the degree of concentration with each erasure. I usually fall asleep while there are still several numbers to go, but in no case have I ever remained conscious more than a few seconds after the last one is gone."

"Exactly," Alan replied. "This process not only relaxes your conscious mind, but it also returns all extraneous thoughts to their proper place in the filing cabinet of the unconscious portion of the mind. Under these conditions your unconscious mind is then able to transmit and receive much more readily than the conscious mind ever does.

"I should, perhaps, be ashamed to admit it, but in your case the temptation was too great to resist, and I am afraid that I ransacked your mind as perhaps no mind has ever been ransacked before.

"I think I can fairly say that I know much more about you than you know about yourself. What I found in your mind was not all that could be desired. Of course, life has been rather harsh with you at times, and I found many scars and a few wounds which are still only half healed. I also found that these same buffetings of fate had given you an unusual depth and breadth of perception and understanding. I decided then that you would be an ideal contact.

"But again we have strayed from the project at hand. I was going to suggest that you use your own method of relaxing your mind. Keep your eyes upon the area of the viewing screen which is now dark. Then when your mind is relaxed, I will attempt to give you a mental picture of the interior of the craft in which you are riding."

It was not necessary for me to visualize a darkened room for, with the viewing beam turned off, the compartment in which I was riding was totally dark. I had no difficulty in visualizing the luminous numerals on the area of the viewing screen, but when I attempted to exclude the dozens of questions which were beating an insistent tattoo upon the fringe of my consciousness, I found it practically impossible.

Eventually I gave up trying to exclude them entirely, swept them as far back as possible, and began to erase the numerals. My mind cleared, so that by the time I reached the last one I was almost asleep.

With the removal of the last numeral, I became aware of a picture upon the viewing screen which I had not noticed before. It did not appear suddenly. It seemed as though it had always been there but that I was seeing it for the first time.

In the left hand portion of the picture I recognized the compartment in which I was riding and I knew that the picture must represent the interior of the entire craft.

4

From New Mexico to
New York and Return
at 8,000 Miles Per Hour

I F I were a writer or a poet I could, perhaps, explain in some magnificent way the spectacular sight which met my eyes as the greatest metropolis in the world rotated slowly before me.

Since I am neither a writer nor a poet, but a technician with a limited vocabulary for expression, I fear that such a description is too difficult to attempt.

As we descended to twenty miles above the City of New York, the lights were much brighter and they had greater individuality. It seemed as though a vast array of millions of blue white diamonds lay scattered before me, scintillating and coruscating against a black velvet background.

The differing temperatures of the various air strata,

combined with the rapid motion of the ship, caused the lights to twinkle violently so that the entire city was a sea of pulsing, shimmering luminescence.

"If I were an artist," I thought, "this would probably be the greatest moment of my life." But knowledge, at that moment, was more important than my desire to express purely aesthetic values.

"Beautiful as this scene is," I thought, "and interesting as this ride has been, I would gladly trade it all for a five minute tour of the mother ship."

"We regret that there was not enough time to arrange such a tour," was the reply. "But you will remember that we are not yet adapted to your atmosphere and, as you yourself said, 'If you were to come into our ship you would have to bring your atmosphere with you.' It is true that, given enough time, we could have prepared a suit such as your people wear when they go beneath the surface of the sea. This would have enabled you to come into our ship without changing either your atmosphere or ours. But this would have required considerable time. While we are not nearly so enslaved by time as your race appears to be, nevertheless, we are aboard a craft which derives its operating energy principally from natural differential sources and, even as men of your race who sail the sea, we often find it necessary to 'sail with the tide.'"

"We must leave this area shortly, but we will return

to your planet within a few months. We have stored enough of your atmosphere to mix with ours for the time we will be gone. When we return we will contact you again."

"But I will not be at the Proving Grounds then," I said. "My work there will be finished and I will have to return to California. Incidentally I don't even know your name, or do you people have given names?"

"We have names," was the reply. "Though there is seldom any occasion to use them among our own people. If I become a member of your race, I shall use the name of Alan, which is a common name in your country and is nearly the same as my given name which is A-Lan.

"As to your being in California; when we return this should make little difference in our ability to contact you. As I said, your mind receives well. In fact, if you had a little more practice in resolving mental images, it might have been possible for us to have shown you the details of our own craft without the necessity of your being in it.'

I heard a voice coming to me but this time as from a distance. Somehow, I knew that it was Alan's voice even though the timbre had changed entirely. The voice I had been hearing had been crisp and rather sharp. This one was soft and flowing, with an almost musical quality.

50

"You are seeing the parts of the ship and its mechanism which your mind is capable of grasping. The large drumlike structure just above the central bulkhead is the differential accumulator. It is essentially a storage battery which is capable of being charged from any of a number of natural energy differentials which may be available.

"For example, in your stratosphere there are layers of ionized gas which, even though they are rarified are also highly charged. By placing the ship in a planetary orbit at this level, it is able to collect, during each revolution, several times the amount of energy differential required to place it in orbit. And it would also receive a continuous flow of high energy electrons from the sun."

"By the word 'charged' I merely mean that a potential difference is created between two poles of the accumulator.

"The material of the two poles has available free electrons in quantities beyond anything of which you could conceive. The control mechanism allows these electrons to flow through the two force rings which you see at the top and bottom of the craft. You are familiar enough with electrodynamics to know that a moving electron creates a magnetic field. The tremendous surge of electrons through the force rings produces a very strong magnetic field. Since the direction and amplitude of flow can be controlled

51

through either ring, and in several paths through a 'single' ring, we can produce a field which oscillates in a pattern of precisely controlled modes. In this way we can create magnetic resonance between the two rings, or between the several segments of a single ring.

"As you also know, any magnetic field which is changing in intensity, will create an electric field which, at any given instant is equal in amplitude, opposite in sign, and perpendicular to the magnetic field. If the two fields become mutually resonant, a vector force will be generated. The effect is similar to, and in fact, identical with a gravitational field. If the center of the field coincides with the craft's center of gravity, its only effect will be to increase the inertia or the mass of the craft.

"If the center of gravity does not coincide with the center of force, the craft will begin to accelerate toward that center. Since the system which creates the field is a part of the ship, it will of course, move with the ship, and without interuption it will continue constantly to generate a field whose center of attraction is just ahead of the ship's center of gravity, so the ship will continue to accelerate so long as the field is generated.

"A very simple analogy would be the small boy who harnesses his dog to his toy wagon, ties a wiener to the end of a stick and holds the wiener in front of the dog's nose. The dog will, of course pursue the wiener, and

so pull the wagon, but because the position of the wiener is fixed with respect to the wagon, the dog will
never overtake it.

"Note that this system does not involve 'free energy'
or what your people refer to as perpetual motion. In
pulling the wagon, the dog is dissipating considerable
energy differential and, while he does not overtake the
wiener, he must be fed regularly if the process is to
continue.

"To slow or stop the craft, the controls are adjusted
so that the field is generated just behind the center of
gravity so that negative accelleration will result.

"You may have wondered how long you could
breathe the air in the small passenger compartment
before it became stuffy and vitiated. You can see here
that there are small vents beneath each of the two rear
seats with a mechanism to circulate the air from the
cargo hold through the passenger compartment.
There is no means, in this craft, of renewing the air,
but the large volume of air in the hold would, in an
emergency, supply even four passengers with adequate
oxygen for many hours.

"The case which you see just above the differential
accumulator contains the control equipment. There
is no particular point in going into this since you are
already familiar with many types of remote control
equipment and servomechanisms. While our controls
are infinitely simpler and more dependable than yours,

53

here again it would require several hours of reorientation in physics to give you an understanding of their operation.

"Our time is running out. We have returned you at a velocity somewhat greater than that of the outward trip and you are now almost directly above your point of departure. Since your people, unlike ours, appear to derive a certain degree of pleasure, or as you call it 'thrill' from experiencing wide variations of gravity, we can, if you wish, produce during the descent, a condition approaching Zero Gravity or what you would term a 'free fall.' To reach this condition fully, would be distressing to anyone, as well as somewhat dangerous, but we can approach it closely enough so that while you will still retain some stability you will experience the sensation of weightlessness."

The sudden realization that the trip was nearly over snapped me out of the state of semi-trance in which I had been since I had first entered the craft."

"O.K.," I said. "Lead on. I'll try anything once."

Instantly the compartment light came on. After that period of total darkness, the light was blinding. While I was attempting to adjust my eyes to the light, my stomach suddenly leaped upward into my chest. For a moment I could plainly feel my heart beating against the lower end of my throat, while my lungs and other upper organs seemed determined to extrude through my ears.

I had been through steep dives and sharp pullouts in airplanes, and have ridden in many amusement devices calculated to produce the feeling of weightlessness, but had never felt anything like this before. There was no sensation of falling. It simply felt as though my organs, having been released from a heavy strain, were springing upward like elastic bands, when released from tension. Fortunately this sensation was of short duration. In a few seconds I felt almost normal again.

"I don't feel very weightless now," I thought, and pushed down sharply with my hands on either side of the seat. I rose in a slow and more or less graceful sweep, almost to the ceiling of the compartment. My rise would have been more graceful except that I had apparently applied the force somewhat to the rear of my center of gravity so that my body tipped forward as I rose and also rotated to my left. By the time I had started to fall back, I was almost head downward and I was forced to reach out and grasp the back of the seat to right myself. The result was that I came to rest with my knees in the chair and my eyes only a few inches from the back cushion.

It was then that I saw something which I had overlooked when I had first entered the ship. It was only a simple design imprinted in the material of the seat, but I recognized the symbol and the recognition must have produced a powerful mental shock wave which

Alan misinterpreted for fear or pain, for the gravity was immediately normalized, causing me to experience another rough moment as my organs all attempted to occupy the space normally assigned to my intestines.

"What is it?" I heard Alan's voice, and for the first time there seemed to be a definite trace of concern. Then—"Oh, I see you have noticed the symbol and recognized its significance."

"Yes," I said. "Anyone who has ever read to any extent would recognize the symbol of the tree and the serpent. It is found in the original inscriptions and legends of every race on earth. It has always seemed to me to be a peculiarly earthly symbol and it was startling to see appear from the depths of space or from whatever planet you call home."

"These are questions which I had hoped to put off until there was more time," Alan replied. "It is difficult even to outline, in a few minutes of discussion, the events of many centuries. For it has been centuries since we have called any planet home.

"The space ship upon which we live, and work and learn, has been our only home for generations. It is quite large as compared to your ocean going vessels, and we have long since developed technological abilities which make us independent of any planet.

"Our ship is a closed system. That is, all matter within the craft, remains within, nothing is emitted, ejected, or lost from it.

"We have learned simple methods of reducing all compounds to their elements and of recombining these elements in any form which is required for our use. For example, we breathe in the same manner as you do. That is, our lungs take oxygen from the air, and replace it with carbon-dioxide. Therefore, the air in our ship is constantly passed through solutions which contain plant-like organisms which absorb the carbon dioxide and give off oxygen as do the plants upon your earth.

"The plant organisms use the carbon in their own growth. Eventually those plants become one of our foods.

"The dozens of natural cycles through which life is created and maintained on a planet such as yours are all duplicated within our ship. Since the size of the ship which contains our race of people is small compared to the size of a planet, the cycles must move more rapidly and under precisely controlled conditions but in every other respect the cycles of life and reproduction are the same.

"There is of course, some net loss of energy which occurs during these cycles, which must be replaced from some outside source. When we are in the vicinity of a star such as your sun, we can easily collect more energy than we require, just as your planet receives more useful energy from your sun than you are presently using.

"During our occasional interstellar journeys, our

ship may be traveling for several generations in areas which are rather remote from any single star, but we can still collect small but dependable amounts of energy from the millions of remote stars and galaxies. There are also, of course, other sources of energy which are constantly available, such as cosmic ray energy and differences in temperature which are also useable.

"It may be difficult for you to conceive of a race of intelligent beings who spend all of their lives within the relatively restricted confines of a space ship. And, in your limited understanding you may even be inclined to feel pity for such a race.

"We on the other hand, are inclined to feel pity for the primitive races which are still confined upon the surface of a single planet, where they are unable to control many of the conditions around them and become the helpless victims of earthquakes, floods, tornados, tidal waves, blizzards, drought, and other hazards which constantly threaten those who dwell upon the surface of a planet.

"Every aspect of our environment is precisely controlled. The temperature is maintained within a fraction of a degree, the humidity, the atmospheric pressure, and even the gravitational force which we create within our ships are all maintained at the exact point of maximum desirability.

"While our bodies seldom leave the ship, our tech-

58

nology has provided us with almost unlimited extensions of our senses so that, for the purpose of observation, learning and understanding, we can be intimately present at any time, and at any point which we may choose to observe or to visit, provided that the point we want to reach or see is within a few million miles of our ship.

"Through our ability which may seem unusual to you but is quite normal to us we are able to generate and apply simple forces at a considerable distance from our craft.

"Our abilities may be somewhat startling and incredible to some of your people, but they are not as startling and incredible as the scientific abilities your people now have compared to the abilities your own ancestors possessed a few hundred years ago.

"Any scientific or technological ability seems incredible to those who have not yet achieved it because they do not understand.

"You are perfectly correct when you point out that the symbol of the tree and the serpent is a common one in the history and the legends of your planet. It is also common in ours. The explanation is we have, at least in part, a common ancestry.

"Tens of thousands of years ago some of our ancestors lived upon this planet, Earth, there was, at that time, a small continent in a part of the sea-covered area which you have named the Pacific Ocean. Some of your ancient legends refer to this sunken land mass as the 'Lost Continent of Mu' or 'Lemuria.'

"Our ancestors had built a great empire and a mighty science upon this continent.

"At the same time there was another rapidly developing race upon a land mass in the south central area of the present Atlantic Ocean. In your legends this continent has been named Atlantis.

"There was rivalry between the two cultures in their scientific progress. It was friendly at first, but became bitter with the passing years, as each race flaunted its achievements in the face of the other.

"In a few centuries their science had passed the point of development which exists here now. Not content with releasing a few crumbs of the binding energy of the atom, as your physicists are now doing, they had learned to rotate entire masses upon the energy axis. Energies equal to seventy-five million of your kilowatt hours resulted from the rotation of a bit of matter about the size of one of your copper pennies.

"With the constantly increasing bitterness between the two races, and with their constantly increasing command of destructive energies, it was inevitable that they should eventually destroy each other.

"The energies released in that destruction were beyond all human imagination. They were sufficient to cause major shifts in the surface configuration of this planet, and the accompanying radiation was so intense and so widespread, that the surface became totally unfit for human habitation for several thousand years.

"But this discussion must wait until we return. Our time is more than up. Already it is requiring too much energy to keep our ship in its present position and we cannot abandon the cargo craft. It is on the ground now and I will open the door. So long, Dan. Step out and take care of yourself until we return."

* * *

Like a person walking in his sleep, I stepped down from the floor of the craft and stumbled a dozen paces through the sand, then turned back to look.

The door had closed behind me and, as I turned, a horizontal band of orange colored light appeared about the central part of the ship and it leaped upward as though it had been released from a catapult.

The air which rushed in to replace that which had been displaced upward, impelled me a full step forward and almost caused me to lose my balance. I managed to keep my eyes on the craft while the band of light went through the colors of the spectrum, from orange to violet. By this time, it was several thousand feet in the air and, as the light passed through the violet band, the craft disappeared entirely from sight.

A strong sense of depression settled over me then. I felt as though my work and my life had lost all of its significance. A few hours before, I had been a rather self-satisfied engineer setting up instruments for the testing of one of the largest rocket motors ever built.

While I realized my part in the rocket-building program was a small one, I felt that, through my work, I was at least traveling in the forefront of progress.

Now I knew that the motor for those rockets was pitifully inefficient and might soon be obsolete. I felt like a small and insignificant cog in a clumsy and backward science, which was moving only toward its own destruction.

For a long time I stood in the sand, looked from the crumpled patch of brush up to the stars and asked myself—

> Did Alan really mean it when he said they would return in a few months and they would contact me again?
>
> Did he really mean it or was it just a polite parting gesture?
>
> Surely there must be thousands of people in this country with more influence who could be of more assistance to them than I.
>
> I can only wait and hope that, in time, I will more clearly understand.

5

A Report by Alan
to Men on Earth
from Outer Space

O N April 28, 1954, Alan established direct contact with me for the third time. A sense of urgency was in his tone and his words impressed me in a way which I had not experienced in our previous discussions.

He insisted that the message he was about to give me should be made clear so that everyone on our planet could understand it.

He explained that, with my background in research, science, lecturing and teaching, I was well-qualified to follow through on his suggestions.

"You have a personal duty and responsibility,"

Alan said, "to cooperate in the efforts our people are making to help you people on earth to alter their present flow of events, and avert the holocaust which is otherwise inevitable."

In the following pages I shall repeat, word for word, as nearly as my memory will permit, the entire conversation which took place between us, in the hope that the purpose and the message given to me of this group of extra-terrestrial visitors may become as clear and understandable to you, as it was to me.

On that night in April, I had driven from Southern California to my special retreat in the Oregon woods in the hope that a meeting might result. I was in dire need of advice, and I felt that Alan was the best and, perhaps, the only accessible source of the answer I required.

During the preceeding months, I had been under increasing pressure to release a complete report of the first spacecraft landing at the White Sands Proving Grounds.

I was reluctant to do so because I felt it would be impossible to persuade any significant number of persons that the event had actually occurred. And no convincing reason was given to me why I should try.

Most of the members of the human race upon this planet have been reared to believe that the men on earth are the supreme product of the universe, as well as the principal reason for its creation.

The thought that a superior race might exist would upset this pleasant belief. And in their minds, those of us on earth would be placed one step down on the ladder of evolution.

This is a place which the egos of many persons would never allow their reason to accept—no matter how compelling the evidence might be.

I felt that if I were to attempt to furnish such evidence as fact I might lose the professional standing which I had worked so hard to acquire during my years of study and research in the field of engineering. I might also be exposed to public ridicule, and could possibly suffer some loss of confidence and respect among my friends.

I saw no good reason why I should risk such a loss of prestige in an attempt to convince millions of other people of facts which the majority of them would not accept as true.

On the other hand, I had slowly become aware of the fact that during the two previous meetings Alan gave me a considerable amount of advanced technical and scientific date, which had proven to be completely valid and I found it useful when applied to my work as an electronics engineer.

The truth is—I was in possession of scientific information which could be more valuable and helpful to the world than I alone would ever be. Once I realized this I felt I had no right to continue to conceal this information simply because I was afraid of what might happen to me as a result of its publication.

My special retreat in Southern Oregon is at the end of a small dirt road that leads deep into the woods. It is a haven of unspoiled nature where the cares and the troubles of the world slip from the shoulders like a cloak that is no longer needed.

It was here that the previous meeting had taken place, and it seemed to be the logical place to seek another.

I had been absolutely alone for three days, and was beginning to give up hope that a contact might be made when, early in the evening of the third day, Alan's voice came out of the silence in its usual abrupt fashion. "Well, Dan, how much longer are you going to hide your light under a bushel?"

In spite of the fact that I had come eight hundred miles, and had been waiting for three days in the hope of making this contact, I was just as startled as though I had never heard Alan's voice before.

I looked around quickly, half expecting to see someone standing in the shadows. My reason told me no one could be there, but Alan had previously given me a precise and detailed explanation of the electronic beam modulation of the auditory nerve, which permitted such communication over considerable distances.

Finally I recovered enough to make an answer, though all I could say was, "What do you mean?"

"You know what I mean," Alan replied, "in your great book of wisdom and philosophy which you call the Bible, it states that when a man lights a candle, he should not place it under a bushel, but should hold it forth so that all men may be guided by its light.

"We have expended considerable time and patience in the effort to light a few candles among the many nations of your planet. It has been our hope that the light of these candles might grow in brilliance so that they will expose the terrible abyss toward which the peoples of your world are so blindly rushing.

"We have given you information which is both of interest and of value to your people. Why do you keep it to yourself?"

"But what can I do?" I said, "I am not a widely-known individual. How can I reach the public. And who would listen to me if I could?"

"There are people everywhere who are searching for the truth and they will recognize the value of the message regardless of who the messenger may be.

"Write what you have learned from us, in a book. You have already met the man who will publish it. Tell the story through your newspapers, your radio and television stations. If necessary, shout it from the house-tops, but let the people know."

"You don't realize what you are asking me to do," I said. "If I carry out what you say, a few people may listen, but many more will not.

"There are too many people in this world who are not yet ready for the truth. They are afraid of anything which might change the existing order of things.

"If I attempt to make public the information you have given me, I may be faced with scorn and ridicule. Some will call me a liar. Others will say I am a fool. Many will believe I am a charlatan. If I give a statement to our newspapers very few would believe it. Most of them may ignore it entirely, or they will print a distorted version which could make me appear stupid and ridiculous."

Alan's voice interupted and it took on the patient but slightly strained tone of a teacher attempting to explain a simple fact to a somewhat backward student. "Of course you will be ridiculed."

"Ridicule is the barrier which those who are ignorant will erect between themselves and any truth which frightens or disturbs them. They continually deny the truth until someone takes enough time to help them understand.

"Can you name any man of your planet who has ever accomplished anything of great value to your people, who was not ridiculed and scorned by some?

"It is the price which is exacted from every man or woman who moves as much as one step in advance of those who live beside them.

"Consider how difficult it was for Columbus, Galileo, Pasteur and Edison to gain attention at the time they announced their discoveries.

"There is an old saying which I believe should be the opening statement of every book of philosophy—

It is easier to ridicule
Than to investigate
But it can never be as profitable

"Yes, some will call you a liar. Others will call you a fool. If you seek or accept financial assistance, no matter how small, you will be accused of commercialism. Yet the same money is a pre-requisite among your people if you ever desire to accomplish anything.

"There are many problems which you will have to face, but remember that they are by no means peculiar to your position. They have been faced and met by every individual who has ever offered his services and his knowledge to his neighbors in the attempt to advance the culture and understanding of the human race.

"Remember also that you have friends, more friends than you realize. And many new friends will come to you.

"While it is true, that many people fear anything which might change their way of life, there are many others who understand the critical problems that exist in your civilization, and they are searching earnestly and diligently for a remedy.

"Such people will understand your desire to spread the truths I am about to give you. They will give you courteous attention and express a desire for greater

69

knowledge so they will look before they laugh. And for every one who looks and desires understanding, you will have another friend.

"Don't forget what I have told you about the power of thought. When you have friends, you are never alone no matter where you may be. Every mind that is for you will remain with you and respect you. And these additional friends will give you added courage and the ability to overcome any problems that may arise."

"I hope so," I said. "I have a feeling that, if I do as you say, I am going to need plenty of both.

"It has been more than four years since you first contacted me. By now, you should be completely adapted to our environment. Why don't you set your craft down on the White House lawn some morning, ask for worldwide communication facilities, and give the whole world your message at once?"

"Such a simple solution is only wishful thinking on your part," Alan replied. "We have discussed this before. If you think a little, you will see that there are many reasons, both general and specific, why such a course would not be successful.

"In the first place, there is the psychological aspect. If we were to appear as members of a superior race, coming from above to lead the people of your world, we would seriously disrupt the ego balance of your civilization. Tens of millions of your people, in their desperate need to avoid being demoted to second place in the universe, would go to any conceivable lengths to disprove or deny our existance. If we took steps to force the realization of our reality upon their consiousness, then about thirty per cent of these people would insist upon considering us as Gods, and would attempt to place upon us all responsibility for their own welfare.

"Of the remaining seventy per cent, most would consider that we were potential tyrants who were planning to enslave their world, and many would immediately begin to seek means to destroy us.

"If any great and lasting good is to come from our efforts, the actual leaders must be your own people, or it must come from men who are indistinguishable from them.

"It is practical, therefore, to realize that if we were to land our craft near the seat of your government, we would immediately be surrounded and taken in charge by those military forces whose duty it is to protect the heads of your government from any possible danger.

"We would be questioned for hours, perhaps days, before any request we might make would even be given consideration.

"We would then be forced to display our superiority in the realm of the material science.

"Once our superiority in this field had been demonstrated, the military leaders would inevitably adopt the

71

position that it was imperative that their country acquire and 'protect' this advanced scientific knowledge.

"The attitude of your government, in common with the governments of other advanced nations of your planet today, is that all new knowledge, particularly scientific knowledge, is the property of the state. To be withheld entirely, or to be disseminated at such time and in such manner as may seem desirable to those who, at that time, are regarded as the governing body.

"Such an attitude is not the fault of any individual or political faction. It is simply a philosophy of government which developed during the last two great wars upon your earth.

"It was given much impetus in your country by the secrecy which was necessary for the development of your nuclear weapons. But military 'security' should be based on logic and reason. It has become, in many cases, an excuse to conceal whatever might embarrass one or more members of your governing bodies.

"As a matter of fact, most of the tensions which now exist between the many nations in your world are the direct result of this excessive secrecy.

"With that in mind, you must realize that any information which your government might acquire concerning us, our craft, or our knowledge, would be considered the most vital 'military' secret they had ever possessed."

"But let's suppose you did land," I said. "Let's

suppose you did give our country the benefit of your knowledge, wouldn't that tend to prevent the outbreak of another war?

"Surely you don't think us so barbaric that we would attack another country simply because we felt that we possessed the means to conquer it?"

"Not at all," Alan replied. "Let me make my point more clearly. If we were to land in your country, your government would attempt to keep it a secret. But it would not succeed any more than it succeeded in keeping the secrets of its nuclear weapons.

"As soon as the government of the Soviet Union knew that the military forces of the United States had acquired highly advanced technical knowledge, they would decide that their only hope of avoiding complete domination by the United States was to launch an immediate attack.

"Remember the lessons of your Pearl Harbor, and you will more clearly realize this.

"If we were to land in both countries simultaneously, the result would, more than likely, intensify the existing race for armaments. Eventually, it could bring about the very holocaust we are attempting to prevent.

"We will point out the way, and help you to understand the wisdom of love and co-operation. And we will give you such help as we can, but you and the other people whom we have contacted must spread the word and help your world to understand.

"Whether or not your children have any future to

look forward to, will depend largely upon the success or failure of your own efforts."

"I realize the danger to our civilization which the possibility of atomic warfare poses," I said. "Everyone who works in the technical field does. Almost every one of the top scientists of our country has, at one time or another, made the statement that full scale atomic warfare will result in the virtual destruction of our civilization, but no one seems to pay any attention to them."

"That is because they have stated only the problem without offering any solution," Alan said. "Actually, the possibility of atomic warfare on your earth is not the problem, it is merely a symptom and no one has ever cured an illness by treating only the symptoms.

"Your civilization is facing a great problem and, during the last few years, it has become a critical one. Its existence is not the fault of any race, creed or political faction, but is purely the result of a basic weakness in your human nature. The lack of attention and the uncertainty you often feel toward the Supreme Creative Force, and your failure to understand how this great Creative Spirit can be used to help you express more love and consideration toward your fellow human beings.

"It is an extremely simple problem, and like most simple things, its importance has been overlooked by too many of your people. Actually the solution lies in a complete understanding of the problem. In order to help you understand it thoroughly, I will state it in the simplest possible terms.

"Every civilization in the Universe, no matter where or when it originates, develops primarily through the continuing increase in knowledge and *understanding* which results from the successful pursuit of 'science.'

"The word 'Science' has been defined in your dictionaries as 'the orderly, and intelligently directed, search for truth.' Under this definition, the whole of science may be divided into three principal parts; for the purpose of discussion and of achieving a greater degree of understanding.

"The three principal parts may be defined as follows: (1) the physical or material science, which deals with the needs and desires of the physical body of man, and with the nature of the physical universe in which he dwells. In this division are found the subjects known as physics, mathematics, astronomy, chemistry, etc., as well as the manufacture and distribution of the endless number of material products necessary to the well-being, the comfort and the pleasure of man. (2) The social sciences which deal with the relationship which exists between man and his fellow man, and the means by which that relationship may be made successful, productive and progressive. In this division are found the studies of society, government, psychology, the non-material phases of economics etc. (3) The

75

spiritual science which deals with the relationship between man and the great creative power and infinite
intelligence which pervades and controls all nature.
This is the power and intelligence which your people
refer to as God.

"All of the science in the Universe, all of the search
for truth and the pursuit of understanding, will come
under one of these three headings or divisions. We
cannot draw a sharp dividing line between them, because there are times when they will overlap, but the
fundamental laws which govern all three divisions are
identical.

"If any civilization in the Universe is to develop
fully and successfully, each of the three branches of
science must be pursued with equal effort and dili-
gence.

"The Spiritual and Social sciences, however, must
come first. There can be no dependable development
of a material science until you have first built a firm
foundation of spiritual and social science.

"You can easily prove this to yourself if you consider the difference between man and the animal.
Some of your people have said that there is no real
difference. They argue that man is just an animal
that has acquired a greater intelligence than the rest,
and so has been able to achieve a material science.

"As your people grow in wisdom and understanding,
they will come to realize that there are several specific

76

differences between man and any of the animals.

"Animals have no spiritual or social science. Consequently, they have never developed any material science, and never will because there is no dependable foundation upon which a material science can be built.

"A few of your insects, such as the ant and the bee (you call them the social insects), have developed a very rudimentary form of social science, to the extent that they are able to live together in large numbers, work together for their mutual welfare, and have a form of discipline which is common to all.

"As a result, they have developed a limited form of material science and have learned to erect simple structures, and store food against a future time of need. They have no spiritual science, however, and their lack of spiritual science has been a bar to any further development. As a result they have not advanced a single step in thousands of years. And of course, they never will because they have long since reached the limits of the structure which can be erected upon their present non-spiritual foundation.

"Mankind, on the other hand, no matter where or when he may come into being, is endowed with the innate realization that there is an infinite intelligence and a supreme power which is greater than man's ability to comprehend.

"During the many stages of his development, man's attitude toward this power may vary from fear and

77

resentment, to reverence and love. But he has always had the instinctive desire to learn more of the spiritual side of his nature and the creative sphere of this power.

"There are no true atheists among the people of your planet or of any other planet.

"Those who say, 'I don't believe in God,' are men who are in mental revolt against some particular concept of the Deity. Their denial of that concept may be well founded, but in the heat of their emotion or in the surge of their ego, they may say 'If this concept is not valid, then no concept can be.' In their hearts they know better.

"No matter how long or how loudly a man may proclaim his independence and believe in the supremacy of his own mind and being, eventually the moment of truth will come.

"When such a man has exhausted all of his own powers and abilities through sickness, accident, loss of money and friends he will instinctively and automatically begin to seek the aid of the one Supreme Power which all clear-thinking men know has no limitation.

"Thus the importance and eternal truth of spiritual science remains ever-dependable since the very dawn of human intelligence. That is why it must always be regarded as the primary branch of science.

"As the mind of man gains in understanding and his spiritual consciousness evolves, he becomes aware of the fact that only through co-operation with man and the Spiritual Love of what he calls God can he effectively improve the conditions of his daily life.

"Because men on your earth so often are reluctant to obey those spiritual laws, it may take thousands of years before this simple principle becomes a normal, everyday attitude which will express itself continuously in the consciousness of all the individuals in your civilization.

"The Spiritual awareness of this fact brought about the first tribal gathering among your people and represents the beginning of your social science.

"From the foundation provided by the spiritual and social sciences, the necessary foundation for the development of material science emerges and this is the point where solutions to the problems which exist in your civilization begin to be solved more easily.

"Once this is realized, the development of your material science, constantly stimulated by the ever-increasing needs and desires of the human body, progresses according to a logarithimic factor of time. It is not a linear development, but one which constantly accelerates.

"You can easily prove this to yourself if you consider the inventions and material developments which have taken place within the last thirty of your years.

"Compare them with the progress of the previous one hundred years, then compare that with the pre-

79

vious three hundred. Finally compare that progress with the previous one thousand years. You will see at once that the material science on your planet develops at a rate which is constantly accelerating.

"Your spiritual and social sciences on the other hand, progress normally only directly or linearly with time. And even this rate of progress is not always maintained.

"Your material science of today is a huge, massive and towering structure. It grows at an ever-increasing rate, yet it is standing upon, and is supported only by the spiritual and social foundation which is growing at a much smaller rate.

"Your spiritual foundation, especially, is too small for proper support of your material science. And we believe it is important to emphasize this fact—

unless some ways and means are found to stimulate the growth of the spiritual and social sciences on your earth, a time will inevitably come when your emphasis on those matters which are material instead of spiritual will cause your civilization to collapse. Ruin and destruction will then be brought to both the spiritual and social side of your civilization.

"This collapse has occurred before upon your planet and your civilization has now entered the stage where it is likely to occur again.

"Your race is now in constant danger of total destruction by an agency which it has itself produced. Why should a people be menaced by their own creations? Simply because they have not progressed far enough in the spiritual and social sciences to enable them to determine the uses to which their creations shall be put.

"Most of the thinkers of your race are well aware of the danger inherent in the use of nuclear weapons, but there is another aspect of the problem which is not generally recognized. Unless unity is achieved between your nations, the very existence of such weapons will eventually bring about the downfall of your civilization, even though they are never used.

"The truth of this fact can be understood by anyone who will think a little. Civilizations are built and maintained by men of vision who think and work for the future. What man will be willing to dedicate his life and his work to the benefit of generations yet unborn, when the foreseeable future may not extend beyond the next twenty-four hours.

"Unless some lowering of tension can be brought about, within a few decades, the motto of men on earth might be, 'Let us eat, drink and be merry, for tomorrow we may die.'

"Already many articles have appeared in your newspaper and magazines commenting upon the rapid rise of what they describe as juvenile delinquency. Some writers place the blame upon the parents, some upon the schools, others blame the church or the state.

"Actually none of those agencies are especially at fault. The condition is due principally to the fact that the majority of the youth of your generation feel insecure. Any of your psychologists will verify this.

"The insecurity of your youth will manifest itself in many ways, but principally in various forms of protest and revolt against existing concepts, institutions and constituted authority.

"It has been publicly stated by one of your highest government officials that the political and military tension between your government and the government of Russia may continue at its present level for the next forty years.

"This would mean that two more generations of your people would be born and reared under the constant threat of imminent annihilation. No civilization which the universe has yet produced could endure under those conditions."

I interrupted him to say, "I think I understand the problem but what about the solution?

"There are many people who sense the hazard of our present position, but their advice varies. Some say we should halt the development of our material science. Some have even suggested we stop working with advanced conceptions of any sort and prohibit the study of nuclear physics.

"Others go even further. They say we should destroy the material science entirely, 'go back to nature' and live as the animals do."

Then Alan replied, "If you wanted to build a large new building, and you suddenly discovered that, because of a miscalculation, the foundation was not going to be strong enough to support the structure, would you at once begin to tear it down? Not likely. You would, instead, look around you for the ways and the means to enlarge and strengthen the foundation.

"The progress of your material science cannot successfully be halted. Either it will go forward, or it will go back. If it goes back, it will collapse because the principle supporting members will be the first to weaken under a program of retrogression.

"There is nothing that is intrinsically wrong with your material science. It will progress and expand to horizons as yet undreamed of, if only your people will provide a spiritual foundation capable of supporting it."

"And if they do not?" I asked.

"Then your civilization will go down," Alan replied slowly.

"It will destroy itself in a holocaust which will leave few survivors. Those who do survive will have neither the ability nor the desire to rebuild their science.

"In a few generations their descendants will have returned almost to the level of the animal. Then the process of evolution will begin again. In ten or fifteen thousand years another civilization will emerge. It will face the same problems and have the same opportunity for their solution.

"If it fails, it too will go down.

"This is an immutable law of the universe which operates according to the free choice of the race.

"Your race and your culture, however, are not doomed to extinction. They may continue upon their upward course until they have left this danger behind them forever.

"The choice, you see, is yours."

"There is little doubt," I said, "which choice the people would make if they had sufficient *understanding* and they were aware of the constructive and destructive alternatives between which they should choose."

"Precisely," Alan replied. "That is why we are here, and that is why you are here.

"As I said before, our ancestors were a group of survivors of the last complete collapse of civilation on your planet. This was more than thirty thousand years ago as you measure time today, but even then they had developed a material science which was, in some respects, at least, considerably advanced over your present position.

"They followed the natural laws, instead of pitting one against the other as your science does. Their devices, therefore, were much simpler. Yet they could accomplish things which you, so far, have been unable to do.

"They, too, failed to realize the absolute necessity of an equal development of the spiritual and social values.

"A political and social cleft developed between the two principal nations of that era. Friction between the two increased yearly, until at last it exploded into a war of annihilation. Weapons of absolute energy were used by each nation against the other, weapons whose destructive power was a thousand times greater than the Hydrogen bomb which threatens your race today.

"There was no question of victory of defeat. They simply destroyed each other. There were few survivors and the radiation level of the entire surface of the planet had been raised beyond human tolerance. This did not mean that all survivors were doomed to immediate death from the radiation, but it did mean the progressive deterioration of the mental and biological functions. This together with the large number of mutations produced in succeeding generations eventually brought their level of existence down almost to that of the beast.

"On a high plateau, in what is now the country of Tibet, six of our aerial craft landed and a council was held to determine what, if anything, could be done.

"It was suggested that an attempt be made to reach another planet. The aerial craft then in use were capable of traveling in space and had frequently been used to reach elevations of a few hundred miles above the earth. No attempt, however, had yet been made

85

to leap the gulf between the planets and the crew members were far from certain that such an attempt would prove successful.

"The planet, which you now know as Mars, was then in conjunction with the earth and, at that time, the surface conditions of temperature, atmosphere, water, etc., were much better suited for human survival than the conditions which your astronomers report to exist at the present time.

"A vote was taken and the members of the crews of four of the craft elected to take the huge gamble in the hope of preserving, thereby, at least a portion of the culture of the race.

"The remaining crew members elected to remain on earth. They believed that because of the elevation of the plateau on which they were gathered and the comparatively low level of the radiation which existed there, they could continue to live in this area without suffering complete physical or mental degeneration in themselves or their descendants.

"I can see the question forming in your mind, so I will explain that this race had achieved perfect equality of the sexes and both were about equally represented in this council. Of the four craft which essayed the great leap, three arrived safely at their destination. There is no record in our history as to the fate of the fourth.

"For many generations the grim struggle for survival demanded the entire time and energy of the people. These were the dark ages of the new race and we have comparatively little knowledge of this period. The original crew members, immediately after their arrival upon the new planet, compiled a carefully written history of the races of earth, pointing out the reasons for their downfall.

"Throughout the intervening centuries, this history has been carefully preserved. It is known as 'The Great Lesson' and is the first thing which is taught to all of our youth when they begin to prepare themselves for active life.

"As the battle for survival was gradually won, the development of the material science resumed its normal pattern. With the lessons of the past constantly before our people, we have found it wise to always maintain the material values in proper relationship to the more important social and spiritual values.

"We have found that all three of the sciences have the same basic natural laws and we have made great progress in understanding those laws.

"We are now essentially independent of planets. Some of our craft are very large, judged by your standards. They are many times the size of your largest ships. And we have the knowledge and ability to produce all of the necessities and comforts of our physical lives within these craft. And, since we have solved the problem of energy, we have no personal need to land upon any of the planets, except occasionally to obtain raw material for new construction.

"The satisfaction of our physical needs now requires but little time and effort. Consequently, we are able to devote much of our thought and energy to the assistance of those races which have not yet passed the critical point in their development."

"Can you give me some specific instructions?" I said. "Some definite information which I can pass along to anyone whom I can persuade to listen?"

"There is little need to do this," Alan replied. "Your own philosophers, both past and present, have given to your people ample instructions. Ample wisdom to enable them to chart the proper course, if they will only realize the absolute necessity of following it.

"If a man with a blindfold over his eyes rushed toward a cliff, a great effort might be necessary to turn him away from the danger. But, if the blindfold is removed, no further effort is necessary since the man will have the wisdom to turn of his own accord.

"There are many statements in your books of religion and philosophy which show that the great thinkers of your race, down through the ages, have been well aware of the dangers of concentration on material science.

"In the first book of your Bible, there is the story of the Tower of Babel, of a race which had lost sight of the spiritual science entirely and were attempting to reach God by the work of their hands. The attempt ended, of course, in frustration and chaos as such attempts always do.

"The development of the social and spiritual sciences becomes almost automatic if the vital necessity of that development is understood by everyone.

"Reduced to the simplest terms, social science is the study of man's relationship to his fellow man. The spiritual science is the study of man's relationship to what you call God. The indispensable requirement for progress in either of these sciences is a sincere desire for a better understanding.

"One of the errors made in the translation of your Bible was the words 'love' and 'charity' were used when the words of the original text actually meant *'understand'* and *'understanding.'*

"In your Bible, it is stated that the greatest commandment of all is—"Thou shall love the Lord thy God with all thy heart, and with all thy soul, and with all thy mind and with all thy strength.'

"The translation should have been written, 'Thou shalt strive to *understand.'*

"There is no need to command men to love God. If men *understand* God, they will love Him continuously.

"Again, there is the statement, 'Though I speak with the tongues of men and of angels and have not charity (understanding) I am become as sounding brass or a tinkling cymbal.' (I Corinthians 13:1)

"It should be obvious that no matter how fluently a man may speak, his words can have no real meaning unless he *understands* that of which he speaks.

"Your books of philosophy state that man should love his neighbor and forgive his enemies. Our books, however, say that if a man *understands* his neighbor and his neighbor *understands* him, they will never become enemies.

"Understanding your fellow man requires the ability to put yourself in his place and see things as he sees them. There is a great difference between knowledge and *understanding*. Knowledge comes from the head but understanding comes from the heart.

"The vital need of all the people and nations of your world is simple *understanding*. There is little value in a treaty, a pact or a guarantee between governments, if *understanding* is lacking between the people.

"You have developed the means of rapid, worldwide communications through your radio, television, telephone and telegraph. These means of communication should be devoted to a much greater extent to increase the amount of *understanding* between nations. You have a few radio broadcasting stations which have helped in many ways to spread the truth, but they are far too few and the programs they carry consist primarily of propaganda. Propaganda is merely the means of 'selling' another person or nation an idea or a course of action which you believe should be followed.

"What the people of your world must recognize is the needs and desires, the hopes and fears of all the people on your earth, are actually identical.

"When this fact becomes a part of everyone's understanding, then you will have a sound basis for the formation of the 'One World' of which your politicians speak so glibly and your spiritual leaders speak so wistfully.

"The people of your nation, through your government, are spending billions of dollars each year in 'foreign relief.' They are simply treating the symptoms and such efforts at 'relief' will never cure the illness.

"Your country spends tens of billions every year to protect themselves against the global conflict which, if it comes, will only prove that the illness has become fatal.

"If ten per cent of that vast sum of money and effort were spent in helping people understand one another, they would then be attacking the illness itself and, in a few years, the illness would be cured.

"When the industries of your nations are released from the necessity of expending their time and energy to produce the means of war and destruction, they will then have the time and the energy to raise the standards of living of everyone on your earth to a point where there would be complete freedom from want.

"With freedom from want comes freedom from fear

and your civilization would be safely past the critical point in its development.

"Your greatest era, your Golden Age, lies just before you. You have only to go through the proper door. When you increase your *understanding,* you will speed up the time when that Golden Age will be reached.

"I have given you as much information and instruction as you are capable of absorbing at this time. As I said before, we have no desire to force our knowledge and our culture upon your race and we will not do so. Nor can we appear in person before your people until there is substantial evidence that the majority of your people *understand* our motives and desire to meet us.

"I will leave you with a final quotation from your own philosophy,

Examine all things
and
Cling to that which is good

"Good-bye, Dan. Do your best. Help people understand the truth about themselves, their existence and their future. When you have made enough progress, we will contact you again."

6

How Do They
Communicate
With Us from Outer Space?

MANY of those who have read the original report of the White Sands Incident have asked me if the means of communication used by Alan could be described as "telepathy."

The question is a difficult one to answer because of the indefinite nature of the term.

The word "telepathy" is defined in Webster's Dictionary as, "Communication between minds by a means other than ordinary and normal." Since the ordinary and normal means are not listed nor defined, however, the definition obviously leaves much to be explained.

The vagueness of the definition has created in the

minds of many students and most of the general public, the impression that telepathic phenomon cannot be satisfactorily explained in ordinary physical terms.

The result is, telepathy is usually relegated to an area of metaphysics which is beyond definition or understanding by the average individual, and is so detached from reality that doubt is cast upon the veracity of any text in which the term is used.

Nevertheless the word telepathy is coming into more frequent use, and an increasing number of persons, both scientists and laymen are beginning to agree that the term does have basic validity.

One of the best books I have read on this subject is "ESP and Your Super-Conscious," by Dr. Gilbert N. Holloway, Ph.D., who is one of the world's foremost exponents on ESP. This fascinating book explains "telepathy" in an unusually clear manner. It also explains the subject of Extra Sensory Perception and how it is accomplished.

Dr. Holloway's book then points out why our government, our schools and universities, should make a deeper study of ESP and shows how ESP can be used to contact our own astronauts in outer space. Then he explains how and why the men in the "flying saucers" have developed ESP to a high degree. In fact, Dr. Holloway's book helps to support and make much of the information contained in this present book more clear.

The results of tens of thousands of specific tests, made under rigidly controlled conditions, leave little room for doubt that transmission of thought, and of specific data, directly from one mind to one or more other minds, does in fact occur, to some extent and under some conditions.

But, while thousands of man-hours of effort have been devoted to the task of demonstrating the fact that transmission of thought can and does take place, little effort has been directed toward the discovery of the actual means by which the transmission and reception are accomplished.

It is presently known that all of the motor and sensory functions of the body are electrical in nature. The entire nervous system of the body is, in fact, a mass of exceedingly complex electrical circuitry.

Continuing studies have shown that almost every function which can be performed by any electrical or electronic circuit is going on somewhere in the human body.

The modulated galvanic currents produced in the brain have been studied for some years through the use of the electro-encephalograph. But it is not so well known that these modulated currents which use the nerves as their conductors, also produce electromagnetic waves (as do all modulated currents when moving through conductors). These waves can, by the use of sufficiently sensitive equipment, be detected, amplified, and displayed upon the tube of a cathode ray oscilloscope.

Since it has been shown that the human system has built-in equipment that creates, modulates and emits radio waves, it is reasonable to assume that it may also contain equipment for the reception and translation of this type of radio wave.

In the communication which took place between Alan and the author of this book, the words spoken by Alan were as sharp and clear as though the speaker were within a few feet rather than being many miles away as was actually the case. (Dr. Holloway points out how easily this can be done to those who know how in the aforementioned book, "ESP and your Super-Conscious.") *

On the occasion of the second contact, Alan made a partially successful effort to explain, in terms understandable to me, the mechanics of the communication system which was being used. He began by pointing out that the brain cannot perceive the sound waves which strike the ear until the mechanism of the ear has converted the sound waves into minute galvanic impulses which travel inward upon the auditory nerve from the ear to the brain.

In fact, the entire function of the ear mechanism is the conversion of sound waves into the tiny electrical

---

* *Published by Best Books Inc.*

currents which are the only impulses that the brain can perceive. He also explained that the human body can, and does, absorb radio waves, and because of its slightly different mass and dimensions, each body will come into resonance with such waves at a certain precise frequency which is typical of that body.

The system used by Alan for the purpose of communicating with the Author, consisted of a beamed carrier wave, tuned to the precise frequency of the individual who is to receive the signal.

The voice modulation is impressed upon the carrier in somewhat the same manner as our radio broadcast stations impress the audio signal upon the radio-frequency carrier wave.

When the receiving body is in resonance with the carrier wave, a small, but adequate portion of the audio signal will be generated, not only upon the auditory nerve, but also upon several other nerves which extend to various parts of the body, but terminate in or near the auditory center of the brain.

The process can be described as "electronic modulation of the auditory system." The end result is, the individual on the receiving end "hears" the spoken word in the same way as though the original sound waves were reaching his ears.

Since the body is in resonance with the carrier, a part of the wave will be re-emitted by the body, and this return wave will be modulated to some extent by the nerve currents generated in the brain of the receiver, when a reply is formulated to the original signal.

Thus two way communication is possible even though the carrier wave is generated at one end of the system only.

Our radar systems can be used as a rough analogy. Here also a wave is emitted in a certain direction by a beam transmitter. Any object in the path of the wave will reflect a portion of it back towards the transmitter. These return signals are then picked up by the transmitting station, amplified and displayed upon a cathoderay tube so that the size, shape and general nature of the object may be determined.

While the system used by Alan is considerably more precise and somewhat more complex than our radar systems, it is a device which could, with a little study, be readily understood and probably be duplicated by our own technology.

There is, however, considerable doubt that such systems would be desirable. And it is unlikely they would contribute to our welfare during our present limited stage of development.

As we know more, we will *understand* more. Then our wisdom and common-sense will increase.

7

Logical Answers
to the Many Questions
about U. F. O.'s

As I travel around the United States and Europe lecturing on unidentified flying objects, I have made a practice of asking the audience if they have any questions. As a general rule, the questions all fall into one general list and this is an attempt to briefly answer some of the questions most commonly asked.

Almost everything I have seen written on the subject of Unidentified Flying Objects has been set down by a member of one or two rather distinct groups of individuals.

One group consists of enthusiastic believers who, in their enthusiasm, are inclined to accept virtually all reported data at its face value.

The opposing group is composed principally of skeptics who look down their noses in a somewhat authoritative and superior way.

Each writer writes his article or book from his own viewpoint, and primarily for the purpose of justifying his own position and belief. A considerable amount of bias is expected and it is always found in such a work.

If it is possible to obtain a completely unbiased and unemotional consideration of the subject then the application of dispassionate logic to the many questions which arise might result in information of considerable value and, thereby, reduce the degree of public confusion brought about by the continuous and, oftentimes, acrimonius debate between the exponents of the two extremes.

The positions of the opposing groups are essentially as follows:

The first group believes and attempts to demonstrate that there is ample evidence to warrant public acceptance of the postulate that the earth is, from time to time, being observed and/or visited by intelligent beings who are not indigenous to this planet.

If this assumption is true, then obviously the scientific progress of such a race would be considerably beyond the level which we have achieved. Their culture could therefore make valuable contributions to ours and we should make every effort to establish continuing contact with such beings for the sake of our own welfare and development, if for no other reason.

Members of the second group usually insist that all of this is nonsense. They state that no reliable evidence exists to prove that intelligent beings have ever visited the earth from any other place and, even if such beings exist, they are certain to be much too far from the earth to have any interest in either observing or visiting this planet.

This group also contends and tries to prove that all reports of U. F. O. observation can, by proper manipulation, editing, and judicious excision of the reported data, be adequately explained in terms of earthly phenomena.

Yet, in any controversy where diametrically opposed views contend with each other, the truth will usually be found to be about midway between the two extremes.

It is not the purpose of this chapter to argue on either side of the controversy, but to examine as fairly as possible some of the many questions which arise.

Whenever an unfamiliar object (U. F. O.) is observed in our skies and the nature and performance of the object cannot readily be correlated to the nature and performance of any known earthly object, the possibility will be expressed by some that it might be a space ship bringing visitors from some other planet.

Such a suggestion does not meet with the approval of certain individuals who, in an egocentric way, believe that man is all important and nothing can equal or surpass man. They try, therefore, to deny and refute any such possibility.

Most of us have been born and reared in the self-satisfied belief that the earthman is the supreme product of the Universe as well as the principal reason for its creation. Therefore, the existence of any superior race would invalidate this belief, and would place us at least one step below them. This is a place where the egos of many persons would never allow their reason to take them no matter how compelling the evidence.

There are other individuals, however, who are able to accept the possibility of the existence of superior races, but they console themselves with the assurance that such races must necessarily be so far away there could never be any likelihood of a meeting between us.

A considerable percentage of modern scientists fall into this last category. Most of our present day astronomers accept the overwhelming statistical probability of extra-terrestrial life and intelligence. They can accept this probability with perfect equanimity so long as that life remains in its own back yard and at least a few light years away.

But, if any evidence arises which seems to indicate that some of this intelligence from another planet may be observing us from our own stratosphere, then the situation changes at once and the evidence must be explained away at any cost regardless of logic or reason.

That is why there is a great deal of truth in the old saying which states, "The human ego is the greatest single barrier to human understanding."

Ever since our astronauts began to penetrate the fringes of space, a change has gradually come about in the thinking of many people. It has become obvious that the coming generations will be going out into space in a constantly expanding area of exploration and discovery.

If men on earth can do this, then it is possible to consider that other races on other planets may already have done so.

Consequently, an ever growing group of people are able to accept the statistical probability that men on earth are not unique in the Universe, and we may not be the supreme example of intelligent life.

When reports are made of objects in the sky which are difficult to explain in earthly terms, these people then begin to ask questions of themselves and of others who may have an interest in the subject. They do not ignore the report as being ridiculous nor do they strive desperately to create earthly explanations for the reports.

The questions almost invariably follow the same pattern and they are usually asked in the same way by all. Most of the questions people ask me are incapable of being answered in a simple or direct way because the question itself represents an oversimplification of the problem which creates it.

For example, the first question is usually asked in this way. "If some of these Unidentified Objects are actually machines, created and guided by intelligent beings not of this earth, where do they come from?"

The manner in which the question is phrased makes it obvious the questioner is thinking in terms of a single possible source whereas the general consensus of scientific opinion today is there are at least a few thousands, if not tens of thousands, of planets in our galaxy alone and each of these may support intelligent beings many of which may have achieved a level of scientific development beyond all possibility of our present comprehension.

There are many evidences of the almost universal acceptance of this postulate by men of science. One of the most explicit was a news item carried by the Associated Press on September 13, 1964. It originated in Pasadena, California, and read as follows, "Creatures as intelligent as man may inhabit thousands of planets in our own 'Milky Way' galaxy a high ranking scientist said Saturday.

"Conditions favorable to life may be far more plentiful than generally thought possible," Harrison

Brown, California Institute of Technology Geochemist, said after a study financed by the National Aeronautics and Space Administration.

Estimating that there may be hundreds of millions of planets in the Milky Way and that many of them are likely to be bathed in life giving light from their suns, Brown said, "One might conclude that man is not alone in this galaxy. Searching for evidence of such intelligent life forms may indeed prove to be profitable and exciting."

Note that the foregoing report is not simply the opinion of one scientist. It is the result of a rather extensive study of the question and a survey of the opinion of the scientists of the world. Thus we see that our reluctant and grudging acceptance of a single possible source of extra-terrestrial life must be expanded to embrace a galaxy which may teem with life and intelligence in every direction.

So it is obvious that the question, "Where do they come from?" can only be answered if specific information has been obtained from the travelers themselves.

The second question is a multiple one and it deals with the logistics of space travel. "How can they cross the almost inconceivable distances between the stars when such a journey would require a number of years even at the velocity of light? What would they eat? How could they breathe during this extended period in space? How can they survive the extreme accelerations which their ships have been reported to undergo?"

These and dozens of other questions of the same sort all relate to the fact that the space travelers, if they exist, must certainly have acquired many abilities which we do not understand and are, at this time, unable to duplicate.

The answer to these questions is simply that the possession of extraordinary abilities would be normal and predictable in any race which had progressed beyond our state of development, just as our scientific abilities are enlarged and extended with each passing year.

It is generally accepted as an astronomical fact that our sun is a relatively new star even in our own galaxy and its planets, including our little earth are comparatively young among astronomical bodies.

It would seem, therefore, to be a statistical certainty that many, if not most of the inhabited planets in this galaxy, contain races which have had much longer periods of development than we, so they can be expected to possess many powers and abilities which we have not yet achieved nor even yet imagined.

The third series of questions deal with the actions which should be expected of newly arrived visitors from outer space. The questions usually begin as follows. "If any of these observed objects are actually space craft created and guided by extra-terrestrial beings, why do they not make their presence known in some unquestionable manner? For example, why don't they land on the White House lawn, step out of their space craft and say, 'Here we are, you lucky earth people, we've come to take over your backward planet and straighten out the terrible mess you've made of things.' "

Other people will ask, "Why don't they land at the Pentagon and seek to establish trade agreements so that commerce might be established between the two races?"

Still others will point out that if the visitors have acquired scientific knowledge and abilities which are greater than our own then, in all probability, they also possess superior weapons which we could not hope to resist. There would be no need for them to trade with us, since they could easily take whatever they might need or want.

Instead of attempting to answer all of those questions separately, we can create a simple analogy to illustrate the position in which the visitor would find himself.

The analogy is easy to understand. And it should enable every reader to answer all of the above questions without further explanation—especially if we can assume such visitors from outer space have developed a higher degree of technical knowledge than our own.

We will begin by recalling the fact that there are,

upon this planet, at least two areas, one in South America and one in Central Australia, where there are still races of people who have not yet achieved the bow and arrow. These tribes actually live in a manner reminiscent of the Stone Age and, from the standpoint of scientific development are many thousands of years behind us, even though they live in areas which are only a few hours by air from our centers of civilization.

We know a little about these tribes because a few of our explorers and missionairies have penetrated briefly into the center of their domain and the reports they have written are available to anyone who is interested.

The most primitive races, on the other hand, have no written language, no means of mass communication and no means of perpetuating information. Consequently, as a race, they know nothing whatever about those of us who live in more progressive areas and they would be unable to understand how we live and what we know, even if they were told.

We do, however, have jet aircraft which can and do fly over the areas in which these people live and, occasionally, our planes may be seen by them.

Let us picture a tribal village nestling in a jungle which is bordered on one side by a large rolling plain. Imagine one of the hunters of the village has wounded an antelope and has pursued his wounded quarry for several miles out onto the rolling plain.

While he is there alone, a large jet aircraft roars

overhead at a fairly low level.   After a few minutes, he
will rush excitedly back to his village with the incredible story of his experience.

"Friends," he might say, "When I was out there on
the plain today, a gigantic bird flew overhead.   Nothing like it has ever been seen before.   It must have had
a wingspread of several hundred feet.   His wings and
all of his huge body gleamed in the sunlight as though
they were made of silver.   As he flew he made a thun-
derous roar that seemed to shake the ground as he
passed overhead and a long stream of black smoke
kept pouring from his tail."

At this point in his story his friends would shake
their heads sadly and his best friend would say softly,
"Please calm down.   Why don't you go back to your
hut and sleep it off?   We knew that fermented juice
would get to you sooner or later, but you insult our
intelligence.   We know all the birds in this area, we
have watched them and hunted them all for years.

"The biggest bird is the Condor.   It has a wingspread of 8 or 9 feet.   No bird ever had a wingspread
of a hundred feet.   And we know that birds have many
different colors, but no bird was ever all silver in color.
Different birds make different sounds but no bird ever
made a continuous roar that shook the ground.   Even
the lion can't do that.

"Everything you said is contrary to what we know to
be true, yet you make your story even more ridiculous

109

by saying that smoke was coming from the bird's tail. How silly. Go back to your hut until you have regained some semblance of sanity, then we'll talk about other things."

The result of such a report would be that no serious consideration would be given to the hunter's story. It would be dismissed as halucination or pure fantasy.

Suppose, however, that a few days later, another hunter should come breathlessly into the village and say, "I just saw one of those big birds too."

If these sightings occurred often enough, eventually it would come to be accepted that perhaps there really was something strange flying overhead and, for the first time, there would be public speculation as to what it might be.

At this point, one of the more thoughtful natives might venture to suggest that instead of being a bird, it might be a machine. This would be a difficult idea to express. The tribe has no word for machine in their language because they have no machines. Nevertheless, the thinker might be able to express the idea that, somewhere in the world, there might be a race of human beings who have developed so far beyond us they can actually build things in which they can fly.

It would be a tremendous idea and hard for the average native to grasp. His friends would scratch their heads and say, "I don't know. It's a far out idea. You're talking about people making things which are impossible. Even if what you say were true, it wouldn't be a logical explanation for the things you say you have seen in the sky.

"It is obvious that if those things were machines and there were people in them, they would look down and see our village. They would want to land their machine in the middle of our village and leap out with a shout 'Take me to your chief. We want to establish commercial relations so that we can enter into trade with your people. We want to get some of those lovely bones which your people wear in their noses, some of that copper you wear about your necks and some of those luscious grub worms you had for lunch.'

"None of the big birds have ever landed in the village so it is illogical to suppose that there might be intelligent beings within them."

Another of the thinkers of the villagers might then interrupt to point out that any race of human beings which could build machines in which they could fly, would certainly possess weapons far more sophisticated and deadly than the spear and stone knives of the village hunters.

"Why should they trade with us?" he would ask. "They would simply land, conquer us, make us slaves, and then they could take anything they wanted. But they haven't done this either so you are right it is illogical to suppose there might be intelligent beings within the big birds."

111

The logic of the villagers is perfectly sound from their own viewpoint. They simply assume that we would do the same things they would do if they were in the plane. The only error in their logic lies in their failure to realize that we no longer wear bones in our noses, and if we want to eat we need not choose grub worms but go into the nearest super-market and choose a wide variety of food completely unknown to them.

As to the super weapons, we do have them, of course, and we could, if we chose, easily conquer the primitive tribe. There is no earthly reason, however, why we should do so since we do not need and could not use any of their possessions or products. They could not contribute anything to improve our welfare and they would become just one more nation to which we would have to ship "foreign aid" every month.

The aboriginal village is not in the least danger of invasion by us, nor is it likely to become a center of commerce.

If any members of our race should visit the village they would probably go only as missionaries in the service of humanity and they would offer such portions of our culture as might be useful to the villagers and which might be accepted by them.

If the missionaries wished to avoid being cooked in the village stewpot or becoming offerings to the village gods they would have to proceed slowly and carefully.

If an advanced race upon another planet decided to

send missionaries to our planet earth, they would be well advised to proceed in the same way. In fact, a careful reading of the front pages of our metropolitan newspapers would be enough to cause them to give up the project as too difficult an undertaking and they would leave for home at once.

The attempt to apply generalities to the U. F. O. reports results only in increased confusion since each report is a separate and distinct event which must be judged strictly upon its own merits.

No study of U. F. O. phenomena will have any value or significance unless the student leaves his ego and emotions in the cloakroom before entering the study hall and even then the only firm conclusion which the student can reach is that no firm conclusion can possibly be valid in an area where the possibilities are as infinite as the Universe itself.

8

What Others Say

DR. J. ALLEN HYNEK, astronomer at Northwestern University, has investigated U. F. O.'s (unidentified flying objects) for the United States Air Force for 18 years.

Dr. Hynek says,* "I have too many sincere and intelligent people tell me, almost apologetically, of seeing something they could not explain.

"I think it is about time for us to ask: 'which are the 25 best-authenticated cases of U. F. O.'s then ask the Government to appoint a panel of astronomers, physicists, psychologists and other experts to evaluate them.

"After all, this craze has been going on for almost 20 years. Its persistence, itself, deserves scientific evaluation.

"It would make the public feel better to see a scientific method applied thoroughly.

---

* U S. News and World Report, April 11, 1966 (pages 14–15).

"Ridicule is certainly not scientific."

* * *

Brigadier General John A. McDavid, USAF, Director of Communications—Electronic for the Joint Chiefs of Staff, said in an Air Force approved speech given at Milliken University, Decatur, Illinois, "We must be prepared for the future. Our relation to other life in the universe is a part of this future, for as the British interplanetary scientist and author, Dr. Arthur C. Clarke, believes, 'There can be little doubt we will ultimately come into contact out in space with races more intelligent than our own.'

"Before long, people may be forced to realize and accept as a fact that this earth is only an infinitesimal grain of sand in an infinite universe, and our human life on earth is only one of many forms of life with which God is concerned and there are others which are in many ways superior to us.

"And, if this is true, our meeting with other types of existence in other places in the universe quite likely will increase the potential element of conflict rather than reduce it.

"This imposes an even greater burden of leadership on our present and future generations."

* * *

The Reverend F. Vera Hodge, vicar of the Church of England, was awarded the military cross in 1943.

115

In an appeal to his 5,000 parishioners he said, "I believe in these 'flying saucers.' Although I have never seen one myself, I feel it is a good thing to hear of them and accustom ourselves to the idea of visitors from outer space.

"Then when they do land in numbers, which I believe is quite likely, we can accept them as friendly visitors, and not grab a gun and start a terrible war with people who are probably more peace-loving than ourselves.

"I think the owners of these flying machines, probably from Venus or Mars, are concerned that we are liable to blow ourselves to bits and, at the same time, we may in some way damage other worlds."

Mrs. Hodge said," I agree with my husband that people should be prepared to expect a landing on earth by beings from other planets. If a martian should land in our back garden this afternoon, I would do as I always do with visitors—invite him in for a cup of tea."

* * *

The Reverand Yasuo Sakurai, President of Oomato (Universal Love and Brotherhood Association), gave an address in Tokyo on August, 1962, in which he said, "The whole of creation is actively one great life body based on cosmic creative will.

"Moreover its activity obeys an established law, and an existence without law is not permissible.

"In view of such a great universe where lawless activities and existence are not permitted, we must adapt the human society to the conceptions of the guiding principles of world federation.

"Man's life has been given by God, Who is the Creator of the Universe. This life bestows equal dignity. To mar this, or to take this away is the utmost felony.

"When we reflect on the past history of human society according to this basic principle, we must admit the fact that a great deal of blundering has been committed.

"Moreover, man cannot live alone. As long as lives of others are dependent upon him, his existence is only possible by the aid of other powers, such a social structure as will mutually exist for all members should be created.

"Herein lies common morals, and a regulation by 'law' for the principle of live and let live should be stipulated. But the morality and the 'law' should not be such as distort or suppress man's life.

"It is love and wisdom that lie at the root of human activities, and the growth and conservation of life and the development of vital power make progress by them. Love and Wisdom must not become egoistic, but be universal love and altruistic.

"In the human community, social peace cannot be realized without the priority of universal love. Therefore, human society ought to adopt 'natural law' based upon the cosmic principles as its foundation of law, and universal love attained by love and wisdom. In this way, universal love and brotherhood can be morally observed as a common criterion. This attitude will then create 'justice' in human society."

* * *

Dr. Holloway, on page 34 of his book, "ESP and Your Super-Conscious" writes, "My ESP indicates that the flying saucer story is not ended. In fact, the study of UFO's has hardly begun, and will gain tremendous momentum as the twentieth century moves forward and evolves toward its resounding climaxes.

"Should you wake up some morning, look out the window and see the sky filled with UFO's, do not fear them. Instead, you should wonder what great manifestations will soon occur in the chancellories of mankind. They can turn out to be the best hope for mankind. And the Forces of the Christ Light will use them in ways beyond our present ability to understand so that we may preserve what is worth saving of our present spiritually weak civilization."

* * *

There are numerous passages in The Bible which hint either directly or indirectly of visitation from space, especially when one considers that writers of that time describe what they see in the language of their own era and that the clouds, fiery chariots and pillars of fire could well have been in their day what we refer to, today, as flying saucers, unidentified flying objects and extra-terrestrial spacecraft.

Following are some of the passages from the Bible which many scholars regard as proof that unidentified flying objects existed several thousand years ago in Bible days and are similar to so many which are seen so often today:

"As I looked and behold, a whirlwind came out of the north, a great cloud, and a fire unfolding itself, and a brightness was about it, and out of the midst, thereof, as the colour of amber, out of the midst of the fire. Also out of the midst, thereof, came the likeness of four living creatures.   And this was their appearance; they had the likeness of a man."—EZEKIEL 1:4–5

"This was the appearance of the likeness of the glory of the Lord.   And when I saw it, I fell upon my face, and I heard a voice of one that spake.   And he said unto me, Son of Man stand upon thy feet, and I will speak unto thee."—EZEKIEL 1:28 and 2:1

"Again I lifted my eyes and saw, and behold, a flying roll.   The length thereof is twenty cubits and the breadth thereof ten cubits."—ZECHARIAH 5:1–2

"Lo, the star which they saw in the east went before them till it came and stood over the place where the young Child was."—MATTHEW 2:9

119

"Behold, there appeared a chariot of fire and horses of fire and parted them asunder, and Elijah went up by a whirlwind into heaven."—2 KINGS 2:11

"Who are these that fly like a cloud, and like doves to their windows?"—ISAIAH 31:5

"Then said I, O my Lord, 'what are these.' And the angel that talked with me said unto me, 'I will show you what they are.' And the man that stood among the myrtle trees answered and said, 'These are they whom the Lord has sent to walk to and fro through the earth.' "—ZECHARIAH 1:9–10

"And when he had spoken these things, while they beheld, he was taken up; and a cloud received him out of their sight. And while they looked steadfastly toward heaven as he went up, behold, two men stood by them in white apparel, which also said, 'Ye men of Galilee, why stand ye gazing into heaven? This same Jesus which is taken up from you into heaven, shall so come in like manner as ye have seen him go into heaven.' "—THE ACTS 1:9–11

Note—all of the above quotations are taken from the King James Version of the Bible.